THE PATH

TO

$1,000,000,000,000

Why U.S. Military Spends So Much Money, where Billions Disappear into and What They Don't Want You to Know

HAWKIN B. KENTON

Copywrite @ 2024 by **Hawkins B. Kenton**

All rights reserved

No part of this book be reproduced stored in a retrieval system or transmitted I any form or by any means, electronic mechanical, photocopying recording scanning or otherwise without the prior written permission of the publisher

Table of Content

INTRODUCTION	2
CHAPTER ONE	6
Understanding The Scale	6
CHAPTER TWO	28
Following The Money	28
CHAPTER THREE	58
Global Military Presence	58
CHAPTER FOUR	78
The Technology of War	78
CHAPTER FIVE	90
The Defense Industry Reality	90
CHAPTER SIX	108

The Political Machine	108
CHAPTER SEVEN	125
Balancing The Books	125
CHAPTER EIGHT	144
Future Perspectives	144
CONCLUSION	168

INTRODUCTION

Have you ever wondered what $916 billion looks like? In the five seconds it took you to read that question, the U.S. military spent more than your car is worth. By the time you finish this page, they'll have spent enough to put multiple students through college. And here's what will really make your jaw drop - some of that money just vanished. Literally vanished. Billions of dollars' worth of military equipment and assets - gone. Even the Pentagon's own accountants can't find them.

But that's just the beginning of the rabbit hole.

Did you know there's a missile that used to cost $25,000 but now sells for half a million dollars? The exact same missile. No improvements. No upgrades. Just a price tag that mysteriously grew twenty times larger. Want to know why? The answer will make your blood boil.

Imagine a world where a single bolt costs $3,357 when the exact same part sits in a warehouse down the street for $15. A world where fixing a clogged toilet costs $400,000. A world where a single hour of flying one airplane costs more than many Americans make in a year. This isn't science fiction - this is your tax dollars at work.

You might think you understand how the military spends money. You don't. Nobody does - not even the Pentagon. When they tried to track it all, they discovered 61% of their assets were missing. That's not a typo. More than half of everything the military owns is essentially lost in the system.

But here's where it gets really interesting.

Somewhere between the $21 million helicopters and the $13.3 billion aircraft carriers lies a secret world of power, money, and influence that shapes every aspect of modern life. That smartphone in your pocket? The internet you're using? The mouse on your computer? All born in military labs, funded by dollars that disappeared into the largest, most expensive military machine humanity has ever built.

By 2024, this behemoth will crash through the trillion-dollar barrier. But the real question isn't how much money is being spent - it's why. Why does America spend more on its military than the next nine countries combined? Why do we need 800 bases in 80 countries, each with its own Pizza Hut and McDonald's? And most importantly, who's really profiting from all this spending?

The answers will shock you. They'll infuriate you. They'll make you question everything you thought you knew about military spending. And once you understand the truth, you'll never look at the world the same way again.

This isn't just another book about military spending. It's a journey into a maze of money and power that affects every aspect of your life, whether you realize it or not. And by the time you finish reading, you'll understand exactly why those at the top hope you never learn what's really happening to your tax dollars.

Ready to follow the money? Hold on tight. Things are about to get interesting.

CHAPTER ONE

Understanding The Scale

From $850B to $916B: The Current Reality

Numbers have a way of losing their meaning when they get too big. Eight hundred and fifty billion dollars, Nine hundred and sixteen billion dollars. A trillion dollars looming on the horizon. These figures float through news headlines and policy discussions, but their true scale remains stubbornly abstract. Yet understanding this scale isn't just an academic exercise - it's crucial to comprehending how America projects power across the globe.

Let's start with a startling fact: the U.S. military's current budget of $916 billion exceeds the entire economic output of Switzerland. Not just Switzerland's military budget - everything the country produces in a year. Every watch, every bank transaction, every chocolate bar, every tourist dollar. All of it. And still, America's military spending is larger.

This mammoth budget didn't appear overnight. In 2022, military spending stood at $850 billion - already an astronomical sum that dominated global military expenditure. But then something remarkable happened. In just one year, that number jumped by $66 billion. To put that increase in perspective, that single year's growth is larger than the entire military budget of most nations. The Pentagon needed $12.6 billion just to offset inflation's effects on its purchases - a figure that alone exceeds many countries' total defense spending.

The scale becomes even more mind-boggling when compared to other military powers. China, often portrayed as America's primary military rival, spends approximately $230 billion on its military - barely a quarter of U.S. spending. Russia, with its massive nuclear arsenal and military industrial complex, spends even less. In fact, you could combine the military budgets of the next nine biggest spenders - China, Russia, India, and six other major powers - and their combined total would still fall short of American military expenditure.

But here's where things get truly interesting: this massive spending doesn't correspond to the size of America's armed forces. The U.S. military employs about 3.4 million people total, including active-duty personnel, reservists, and civilian employees. China and India both maintain larger military forces. Yet somehow, these fewer American personnel require vastly more funding than their counterparts anywhere else in the world.

The numbers become even more striking when broken down into specific expenditures. The military spends $2.5 billion solely on offsetting increased fuel costs. A single weapons program, the F-35 fighter jet, will ultimately cost taxpayers $2 trillion - more than the GDP of most countries. One aircraft carrier runs $13.3 billion, requiring 49 million hours of labor to construct. Even seemingly minor items carry astronomical price tags - each cruise missile costs $1.6 million, and the military ordered 600 of them last year alone.

This explosive growth in spending continues despite the conclusion of major conflicts. The withdrawal from Afghanistan, the end of the Iraq War - none of these developments has slowed the budget's relentless expansion. Instead, the numbers keep climbing, driven by forces that seem to operate independently of actual military engagements or requirements.

What makes this trajectory even more remarkable is how it persists regardless of economic conditions. During times of recession, most government departments face budget cuts. During peacetime, military spending typically decreases. Yet America's military budget defies these normal patterns, growing year after year with seemingly unstoppable momentum.

Consider the maintenance costs alone. The Department of Defense spends $352 billion annually just on operations and maintenance - a figure larger than the entire economy of Portugal. This includes everything from keeping bases running to providing healthcare for active-duty personnel, from environmental cleanup of military sites to disaster relief operations. The sheer scale of these support operations demonstrates how America's military has evolved into something far beyond a traditional fighting force.

Looking ahead, experts predict this upward trajectory will continue. As global tensions rise and new technologies emerge, military spending appears poised to cross the trillion-dollar threshold by 2024. This isn't just speculation - it's based on current growth patterns and already-planned expenditures. The question isn't whether we'll reach a trillion dollars - it's how far beyond that we'll go.

This steady march toward ever-larger budgets raises crucial questions about sustainability, necessity, and the nature of military power itself. As we delve deeper into where this money goes and why it's spent, we'll uncover a complex web of political, economic, and strategic forces that shape the largest military machine in human history.

The numbers may seem abstract, but their implications are anything but. Every dollar represents choices made, priorities set, and resources allocated. Understanding these choices - and their consequences - is essential to comprehending America's role in the modern world. As we'll see, the scale of military spending isn't just about defense - it's about how America defines its place in the global order.

More Than Nine Nations Combined

When people say America's military budget exceeds that of the next nine nations combined, the statement often passes as just another statistic. But let's pause and truly absorb what this means. Russia's massive military machine, China's rapidly modernizing forces, India's vast army, Britain's royal forces, and five other major military powers - add all their defense spending together, and America still spends more.

China, America's nearest competitor, invests approximately $230 billion in its military annually. This seems substantial until you realize it's barely a quarter of America's $916 billion budget. Even more striking is that China maintains a larger standing army than the United States. How can America spend so much more while employing fewer personnel? The answer lies not in the size of the force, but in how the money is spent.

Consider this stark contrast: When China spends money equipping an infantry soldier, the total cost runs about

$1,500, with roughly $700 going to their rifle. An American infantryman, by comparison, costs $17,000 to equip, with the most advanced body armor, night vision equipment, and combat gear available. This pattern repeats across every aspect of military spending - America consistently opts for the most advanced, and consequently most expensive, options available.

The disparity becomes even more pronounced when examining specific military capabilities. Take aircraft carriers - while other nations operate smaller carriers, America maintains a fleet of eleven supercarriers, each costing $13.3 billion. These floating cities represent more naval aviation power than the rest of the world combined. The U.S. Navy's air force is actually the second-largest air force in the world - second only to the U.S. Air Force itself.

Training costs reveal another dimension of this spending gap. American fighter pilots log between 180 to 200 flight hours annually for training. Russian pilots average 60 to 100 hours, and Chinese pilots manage about 110 hours. Each of these training hours comes with hefty fuel, maintenance, and support costs. Operating an F-35 fighter for just one hour runs $35,000 - more than many Americans earn in a year.

The gap extends into research and development as well. The U.S. military spends $140 billion annually on R&D alone - more than half of China's entire military budget. This investment powers everything from artificial intelligence research to autonomous submarines, from laser weapons to exoskeletons that could transform ordinary soldiers into near-superhuman fighters.

But perhaps the most telling comparison comes in how these nations maintain their global presence. While Russia operates a handful of overseas bases and China is slowly establishing its first foreign installations, America maintains approximately 800 bases in 80 countries. Each of these bases requires substantial infrastructure - everything from runways to housing, from hospitals to entertainment facilities. Many even include American restaurant chains and grocery stores, creating little pieces of America around the globe.

This vast network of bases costs about $55 billion annually to maintain - more than the entire military budget of many nations. Yet this expenditure is seen as essential to America's strategy of global power projection, allowing rapid response to any crisis anywhere in the world.

The spending disparity becomes even more pronounced in specific weapons programs. While other nations carefully allocate resources across their military needs, America simultaneously pursues multiple massive procurement programs. The F-35 fighter program alone will cost $2 trillion over its lifetime - nearly seven times China's annual military budget.

This overwhelming spending advantage has created what military planners call "overmatch" - the ability to decisively defeat any potential adversary through superior technology and capabilities. During Operation Desert Storm, American tanks could identify and destroy Iraqi tanks before the Iraqi crews could even see their opponents. This technological edge, however, comes at an astronomical cost.

Yet these comparisons raise important questions. Does this massive spending disparity translate into proportionally greater security? Does maintaining such an overwhelming military advantage actually prevent conflict, or does it spark arms races as other nations struggle to catch up? As China rapidly modernizes its military and Russia maintains its nuclear arsenal, these questions become increasingly relevant.

The reality is that America's military spending reflects not just defense needs, but a broader vision of global leadership. While other nations focus primarily on territorial defense and regional influence, America's military budget supports a system of global order - from protecting international shipping lanes to responding to natural disasters worldwide.

Understanding this context helps explain why American military spending so drastically exceeds that of other nations. It's not just about defending territory or winning wars - it's about maintaining a global system that America helped create and continues to lead. Whether this approach represents the most effective use of resources remains a subject of intense debate, but its scale and scope are undeniable.

The American Paradox

One of the most perplexing aspects of American military spending emerges when you look at personnel numbers. Despite its astronomical $916 billion budget, the U.S. military isn't the world's largest fighting force - not even close. With approximately 3.4 million total personnel, including 1.3 million active-duty service members and roughly 800,000 in reserves and National Guard, America's military is actually smaller than both China's and India's forces. This creates a striking paradox: how does the U.S. military spend so much more while employing fewer people?

The answer begins with how America compensates its service members. As an all-volunteer force, the U.S. military must offer competitive salaries and benefits to attract and retain personnel. This translates to approximately $172 billion spent annually on military personnel costs alone - a figure that covers pay, benefits, retirement, and healthcare for service members and their families. The military has become one of the world's largest employers, providing comprehensive benefits packages that include everything from housing allowances to education benefits.

Yet even this massive personnel budget reveals troubling contradictions. Despite spending billions on personnel, in 2019, approximately 22,000 active-duty service members qualified for food stamps. The situation has become so acute that the Army currently recommends soldiers apply for food assistance to cope with rising inflation. In a budget approaching a trillion dollars, this stark reality raises serious questions about priorities and allocation.

The military's healthcare system alone consumes $39 billion annually, providing medical services for active-duty personnel. An additional $50 billion goes toward various healthcare costs, making the military one of America's largest healthcare providers. When combined with veteran benefits, the United States spends over $250 billion annually caring for current and former service members - more than China, Russia, and India spend on their veterans combined.

Training costs create another significant disparity. It costs the Air Force approximately $10.7 million to train a qualified F-35 pilot and nearly $11 million for an F-22 pilot. For the Army, transforming a civilian into a fully trained infantry soldier costs about $50,000, not including the $17,000 worth of equipment they receive. Compare this to China, which spends roughly $1,500 per infantry soldier, and the scale of American investment becomes clear.

The military also maintains a unique recruitment infrastructure. In 2022, they spent $28 million just on hiring artificial intelligence experts. The Pentagon offers signing bonuses up to $50,000 for new recruits with specific qualifications, and additional bonuses up to $40,000 for current personnel who train in high-demand skills like foreign languages or technical explosives handling.

But perhaps the most striking aspect of this personnel paradox appears in the support structure surrounding each service member. The U.S. military doesn't just employ soldiers, sailors, airmen, and marines - it maintains an extensive network of civilian employees, contractors, and support staff. This includes everyone from teachers in base schools to maintenance workers, from scientists in research laboratories to logistics specialists managing global supply chains.

The military also invests heavily in quality of life for its personnel stationed abroad. Those 800 overseas bases aren't sparse outposts - they're fully functioning American communities, complete with schools, shopping centers, and entertainment facilities. The military flies American products to bases worldwide, ensuring service members have access to familiar brands and comfort foods, regardless of their location. While this might seem extravagant, it's considered essential for maintaining morale and retention in a volunteer force.

This comprehensive approach to personnel support extends beyond active service. The military provides extensive transition assistance for those leaving service, employment support for military spouses, and continuing education opportunities for service members and their families. A significant portion of the $352 billion operations and maintenance budget goes toward these support services.

Yet this creates another paradox: while spending enormous sums on personnel and support services, the military increasingly invests in automation and unmanned systems. From drone aircraft to autonomous submarines, from AI-powered analysis systems to robotic combat vehicles, the trend points toward reducing human involvement in military operations while simultaneously increasing per-person costs.

Understanding this personnel paradox is crucial to grasping how American military spending works. The U.S. has chosen a path of maintaining a smaller, professional force equipped with cutting-edge technology and supported by comprehensive infrastructure. This approach costs more - much more - than maintaining a larger force with basic equipment and minimal support, but it aligns with American strategic priorities and social expectations.

The question isn't whether this approach delivers superior military capabilities - it demonstrably does. The question is whether the massive disparity between personnel numbers and budget allocation represents the most effective use of resources. As military technology continues to advance and personnel costs continue to rise, this paradox will likely become even more pronounced in the years ahead.

The Journey to Current Spending

The path to America's current $916 billion military budget tells a story of continuous expansion, driven by historical lessons and global ambitions. This journey begins with a crucial turning point - America's experience in World War II. Before that conflict, the United States maintained a policy of military isolation, believing that if it avoided attacking other nations, no one would attack America. Pearl Harbor shattered that illusion, teaching a lesson that would fundamentally reshape American military strategy.

From this experience emerged a new doctrine: defeat potential enemies before they can threaten the American homeland. This shift marked the beginning of an unprecedented military expansion that would transform a relatively isolated nation into a global superpower. The

Cold War accelerated this transformation, as America and the Soviet Union engaged in a massive arms race that would reshape military spending patterns for decades to come.

During the Cold War, military budgets reached staggering heights. At its peak, defense spending consumed 14% of America's GDP during the Korean War. Even during periods of relative peace, Cold War military spending rarely dropped below 10% of GDP. Compare this to today's 3.5% - a figure that, while lower as a percentage, represents far more actual dollars due to America's massive economic growth.

The spending race between the U.S. and Soviet Union created a dangerous spiral. Each side's military expansion prompted the other to spend more, leading to an arms race that ultimately produced over 10,000 nuclear warheads on each side. This pattern of competitive spending established a precedent that continues to influence military budgets today, as America works to maintain its technological edge over rising powers like China.

The end of the Cold War briefly suggested a possibility of reduced military spending - the so-called "peace dividend." Military spending did decrease slightly, but only for a moment. The terrorist attacks of September 11, 2001, launched America into a new era of military expansion. The Pentagon's budget swelled to support operations in Afghanistan and Iraq, with war-related costs reaching $160 billion per year through a separate Overseas Contingency Operations fund.

Even after withdrawing from Afghanistan and Iraq, military spending continues to grow. The initial focus on counter-terrorism has evolved into preparation for potential conflicts with peer competitors. China's military modernization, in particular, drives significant spending increases as America works to maintain its technological advantages.

Today's military spending reflects this accumulated history. The U.S. maintains expensive nuclear deterrent forces developed during the Cold War, counter-terrorism capabilities built after 9/11, and increasingly sophisticated weapons systems designed to counter emerging threats. Each layer of capability adds to the budget, creating what military planners call a "full-spectrum force" capable of fighting any type of conflict anywhere in the world.

But this journey hasn't been smooth or efficient. The Department of Defense remains the only federal agency unable to pass an independent audit, thirty years after Congress first required it. The Pentagon's procurement system regularly produces expensive disappointments, like the USS Freedom, a naval vessel that cost hundreds of millions more than planned yet failed to meet basic performance requirements.

The journey to current spending levels also reveals how military expenditure becomes self-perpetuating. Defense contractors strategically locate facilities across congressional districts, creating jobs that make reducing military spending politically difficult. The revolving door between the Pentagon and defense industry creates powerful incentives to maintain high spending levels. What began as a response to genuine security threats has evolved into an ecosystem that generates its own momentum.

Looking at this history helps explain not just how America reached its current level of military spending, but why reducing it proves so challenging. The military budget represents not just current security needs, but accumulated commitments, established infrastructure, and entrenched interests built up over decades.

Yet this journey continues. As America approaches the trillion-dollar threshold, new questions emerge about sustainability and necessity. The costly lessons of past conflicts shape current spending, but they may not provide the best guide for future security challenges. Understanding how we reached this point becomes crucial for deciding where we go from here.

The path to current spending levels reflects America's evolution from a relatively isolated nation to global superpower. Each increase in the budget, each new weapons system, each overseas base represents a choice about America's role in the world. As we look toward future spending decisions, understanding this journey becomes essential for evaluating whether traditional patterns of military spending still serve American interests in a rapidly changing world.

Chapter Two

Following The Money

The $352B Backbone

When most people think about military spending, they envision sleek fighter jets and massive aircraft carriers. But the largest single chunk of America's military budget a staggering $352 billion - goes to something far less glamorous: operations and maintenance. This figure alone exceeds the entire economy of Portugal, and it represents the complex machinery that keeps America's global military presence functioning around the clock.

Behind this enormous number lies a web of daily operations so vast it challenges comprehension. The Department of Defense, one of the world's largest organizations, requires an intricate support system just to function. It's the equivalent of running a global corporation, a massive healthcare system, and a small nation all at once. The complexity is so immense that just creating the report to track these expenditures costs the Pentagon $269,000.

Consider the basic logistics: The military must transport fuel, food, equipment, and personnel across a network of 1,250 bases worldwide. Of these, approximately 800 bases exist outside U.S. territory, each requiring its own support infrastructure. These aren't sparse outposts - they're fully functioning American communities, complete with their own grocery stores stocked with products flown in from the United States, Pizza Huts, McDonald's, and Subway restaurants to make service members feel at home.

The healthcare component alone consumes $39 billion of the operations and maintenance budget, providing medical services for active-duty personnel. This includes everything from routine checkups to combat injury treatment, maintaining military hospitals, and supporting medical staff worldwide. It's essentially running a nationwide healthcare system that must function everywhere from desert combat zones to Pacific islands.

Environmental responsibilities form another surprising portion of this budget. The military must clean up areas where it has left unexploded ordnance or spilled chemicals into local environments. These cleanup operations, while rarely discussed, represent a significant ongoing cost. The military also maintains a disaster relief capability, responding to humanitarian crises worldwide - another hidden but substantial expense within the operations budget.

Training exercises consume another massive portion of these funds. Moving an Armored Brigade Combat Team just one mile costs $66,000 in maintenance and fuel. Multiply this by thousands of units conducting regular training exercises worldwide, and the costs become astronomical. Yet this training is considered essential for maintaining combat readiness and deterring potential adversaries.

The maintenance of military equipment presents its own challenges. Every vehicle, aircraft, and ship requires regular servicing to remain operational. When a single F-35 fighter costs $35,000 per hour just to fly, the maintenance budget must account for not just repairs but the extensive infrastructure needed to perform them. Aircraft carriers, with their 750 bathrooms that can cost $400,000 each to unclog when systems fail, exemplify the unexpected maintenance challenges that drive up costs.

Anti-drug activities consume nearly a billion dollars of this budget, while $10 million goes to security at international sporting competitions. These seemingly peripheral activities highlight how the military's responsibilities extend far beyond traditional combat operations. The operations and maintenance budget must cover everything from counternarcotics operations to protecting high-profile international events.

Perhaps most remarkably, this massive spending occurs despite - or perhaps because of - significant inefficiencies in the system. The Pentagon has never successfully passed an audit, and 61% of their physical assets are effectively missing from their tracking systems. This means they're likely spending money on equipment and supplies they already own but can't locate, creating a cycle of redundant purchases and wasteful spending.

The sheer scale of operations and maintenance spending reveals a fundamental truth about modern military power: maintaining capability is often more expensive than creating it. While procurement of new weapons systems generates headlines, it's the daily cost of keeping existing systems operational that consumes the largest share of military spending.

This reality creates a challenging dynamic. Every new weapons system or capability added to the military's arsenal generates an ongoing maintenance requirement that extends decades into the future. Each new base established overseas creates a permanent need for support infrastructure. The operations and maintenance budget thus becomes a measure not just of current military activities, but of accumulated commitments built up over years of expansion.

Understanding this $352 billion backbone of military spending illuminates why reducing military expenditure proves so challenging. Every dollar serves some purpose, supports some facility, maintains some capability deemed essential to national security. Yet the very size of this spending, and the complexity it represents, raises crucial questions about sustainability and efficiency in maintaining America's global military presence.

The Human Factor: $172B in Personnel Costs

Behind every tank, aircraft, and warship in America's military arsenal stands a human being. The Pentagon spends $172 billion annually on these human assets - a figure that tells a complex story about what it costs to maintain the world's most advanced volunteer military force. This isn't just about salaries; it's an intricate web of compensation, benefits, training, and support that sustains America's fighting force and their families.

Let's put this number in perspective. At 3.4 million total personnel - including 1.3 million active duty service members and approximately 800,000 reservists and National Guard members - the Department of Defense stands as the world's largest employer. The $172 billion covers pay, benefits, retirement packages, and healthcare for these personnel and their families, creating a comprehensive support system unlike any other military force on Earth.

Yet within this massive spending lies a troubling paradox. Despite the enormous budget, many service members struggle financially. In 2019, a shocking statistic emerged: 22,000 active-duty service members qualified for food stamps. The situation has become so dire that the Army officially recommends soldiers apply for food stamp benefits to combat rising inflation. This stark reality raises serious questions about how such extensive personnel spending can coexist with financial hardship among service members.

The cost of maintaining this volunteer force starts with recruitment. The military offers signing bonuses up to $50,000 for new recruits with needed qualifications. Current service members can earn additional bonuses up to $40,000 for training in high-demand skills like foreign languages, psychological operations, or technical explosives handling. Just recruiting artificial intelligence experts cost the Pentagon $28 million in a single year.

Training costs represent another massive investment in personnel. Transforming a civilian into a qualified F-35 pilot costs approximately $10.7 million, while F-22 pilot training runs nearly $11 million. Even basic infantry training costs about $50,000 per soldier, not including their $17,000 worth of individual equipment. These figures dwarf the training investments of other major military powers - China, for instance, spends just $1,500 per infantry soldier.

Healthcare forms a substantial portion of personnel costs. The military operates its own healthcare system, providing comprehensive medical coverage for active-duty personnel and their families. This isn't just about combat injuries - it includes everything from routine checkups to maternal care, dental services to mental health support. The system must function everywhere U.S. troops are stationed, from major bases to remote outposts.

The military's commitment to personnel extends far beyond basic needs. For troops stationed overseas, the Pentagon creates miniature versions of American life, complete with familiar restaurant chains and grocery stores stocking American products. While this might seem extravagant, it's considered essential for maintaining morale and retention in a volunteer force deployed far from home.

Family support represents another significant cost center. The military provides housing allowances, operates schools for service members' children, offers employment assistance for military spouses, and maintains recreational facilities on bases worldwide. These services aim to support not just the service members but their entire families, recognizing that military service affects entire households.

Education benefits form a crucial part of the personnel package. The GI Bill, one of the military's most significant recruitment tools, promises service members the opportunity to attend college during or after their service. The military also offers tuition assistance for active-duty personnel and their families, viewing education as both a benefit and an investment in force capability.

Retirement benefits add another layer of complexity to personnel costs. Unlike most private sector employees, military personnel can retire after 20 years of service with a pension worth 50% of their base pay, increasing to 75% after 30 years. These long-term obligations create financial commitments that extend decades beyond active service.

The human factor in military spending reveals much about America's approach to military power. Rather than maintaining a larger force of minimally supported conscripts, the U.S. has chosen to invest heavily in a smaller, professional force. This approach costs more per person but delivers a more capable, committed fighting force.

However, this spending pattern also creates challenges. As personnel costs continue to rise faster than inflation, maintaining the current force structure becomes increasingly expensive. The military must constantly balance investing in people against other priorities like modernization and readiness.

Understanding these personnel costs becomes crucial for evaluating military spending as a whole. While weapons systems generate headlines, it's the human infrastructure that ultimately determines military effectiveness. The $172 billion spent annually on personnel represents not just current costs but America's long-term commitment to maintaining a professional, volunteer military force.

Innovation Investment: $140B in R&D

The United States military invests $140 billion annually in research and development - a sum equivalent to Morocco's entire economy. This massive investment funds everything from laser weapon systems to artificial intelligence, from autonomous submarines to advanced exoskeletons for soldiers. But while the numbers are clear, the implications of this spending reach far beyond military applications.

The Pentagon's research and development budget operates on a fundamental principle: maintain absolute technological superiority on the battlefield. This investment splits between immediate combat advantages and long-term technological breakthroughs. The military channels billions into artificial intelligence systems that analyze drone footage, enhance targeting capabilities, and develop autonomous systems for future combat operations.

But here's what makes this investment truly fascinating - many technologies we use daily were born in these military labs. GPS navigation? Military technology. The internet itself? Created for and by the Department of Defense. Even the computer mouse on your desk traces its origins to military research. Voice recognition, drones, and countless other innovations emerged from this massive R&D machine.

Consider the current projects under development. The military is testing ship-based laser weapons that sound like they're straight out of Star Wars. They're developing exoskeletons that could allow soldiers to carry hundreds of pounds of equipment without fatigue. Autonomous submarines prowl the depths while AI systems process battlefield data faster than any human analyst could dream of.

Yet this innovation doesn't come cheap. The military's approach to research differs fundamentally from the private sector. While companies typically seek the most cost-effective solutions, military researchers pursue the most capable ones, regardless of cost. When you're developing technology that could decide the outcome of a future war, price becomes a secondary consideration.

The scope of this research extends far beyond weapons. The Pentagon invests heavily in medical research, developing new treatments for combat injuries that often revolutionize civilian medicine. They research advanced materials that could make vehicles lighter and stronger, alternative energy sources that could power bases in remote locations, and communication systems that could function even if traditional networks fail.

However, this massive R&D investment has its critics. Some point to projects like the F-35 fighter jet, whose development costs have spiraled to astronomical levels while technical problems persist. Others note that potential adversaries like China often wait for America to perfect new technologies, then reverse-engineer them at a fraction of the development cost.

Still, the military argues this investment is crucial for maintaining America's edge. In modern warfare, technological superiority can mean the difference between victory and defeat. During Desert Storm, American tanks could identify and destroy Iraqi vehicles before the enemy even knew they were there - a direct result of superior technology developed through years of research.

The Pentagon's research priorities reveal much about how it sees future threats. Heavy investment in cyber capabilities suggests preparing for digital warfare. Research into hypersonic weapons aims to counter similar developments by China and Russia. Work on autonomous systems indicates a future where robots may play an increasingly important role in combat.

Perhaps most intriguingly, this R&D spending creates a unique ecosystem where military needs drive civilian innovation. When the military perfects a technology for warfare, private companies often adapt it for civilian use. The internet began as a military communication network. GPS started as a way to guide missiles. Even everyday technologies like microwave ovens trace their lineage to military research.

Looking ahead, the $140 billion research budget focuses increasingly on emerging technologies like quantum computing, biotechnology, and artificial intelligence. These investments could reshape not just warfare but society itself. As with previous military innovations, today's classified research projects could become tomorrow's consumer technologies.

Yet questions remain about whether this massive research investment delivers proportional returns. While the military's R&D efforts have produced undeniable breakthroughs, they've also generated costly failures and projects that never made it out of the laboratory. The challenge lies in balancing the need for cutting-edge capabilities against the reality of finite resources.

Understanding this $140 billion investment becomes crucial for grasping how America approaches military power. It's not just about maintaining current capabilities - it's about shaping the future of warfare itself. Whether this massive research investment represents the best use of resources remains debatable, but its impact on both military and civilian technology is undeniable.

Procurement Programs: $167B in Equipment

The United States military spends $167 billion annually on procurement - an amount equivalent to Ethiopia's entire economy - to purchase everything from aircraft carriers to basic combat gear. This massive purchasing power translates into specific, tangible military assets that define American combat capabilities worldwide.

Numbers tell the procurement story with stark clarity. In 2023, the military purchased 77 new jets at $142 million each, immediately following up with a request for $14 billion to acquire 83 more. These aircraft require substantial ongoing investment - each F-35 fighter costs $35,000 per hour just to operate. The military ordered 600 cruise missiles at $1.6 million each, spending nearly a billion dollars on these weapons alone.

Ground transportation represents another significant procurement cost. The military purchased 3,700 troop transport vehicles at $372,000 each in one year, then ordered 3,100 more the following year. For naval forces, three destroyer-class ships cost $8.2 billion. The Navy's newest aircraft carrier, the USS Gerald R. Ford, required $13.3 billion and 49 million work hours to construct.

The procurement budget also includes sophisticated helicopter programs. The military allocated $1.2 billion for 56 Black Hawk helicopters and invested $2.3 billion in ten CH-53K King Stallion heavy-lift helicopters. These King Stallions represent the world's most powerful heavy-lift helicopters, capable of delivering supplies, equipment, and even howitzers to troops conducting amphibious operations.

Maritime procurement extends beyond combat vessels. The Navy spent $1 billion on two fleet replenishment oilers and $100 million on a towing, salvage, and rescue ship. These support vessels prove crucial for maintaining global operations, enabling the fleet to operate far from American shores for extended periods.

The evolution of procurement costs reveals troubling trends. The Stinger missile, which once cost the Pentagon $25,000, now commands nearly half a million dollars - a price increase that far outpaces inflation. This pattern repeats across multiple weapons systems, driven by limited competition among defense contractors and increasingly complex technical requirements.

Ammunition procurement itself consumes substantial resources. The military spent $812 million acquiring 4,718 GMLRS (Guided Multiple Launch Rocket System) rockets to replace those provided to Ukraine. The Patriot missile system required $1.037 billion for 252 missiles and associated launch platforms, split between replacing donated inventory and strengthening facilities abroad, particularly in the Pacific region.

Modern warfare's technological demands drive significant investments in unmanned systems. The military allocated nearly $3 billion for various drone programs, including the Triton, Stingray, and Reaper platforms. A specialized program received $200 million to develop stealthy drones providing direct overwatch and fire support for special operations forces.

Naval aviation procurement remains particularly costly. The E-2D Advanced Hawkeye program consumed $1.3 billion for five aircraft, providing critical early warning radar coverage and command and control capabilities for naval operations. These specialized aircraft extend the fleet's surveillance and coordination capabilities by hundreds of miles in every direction.

The procurement process itself faces significant challenges. Many major weapons systems receive bids from only one contractor, eliminating competitive pressure to control costs. The Pentagon often finds itself locked into specific suppliers for maintenance and upgrades, creating long-term dependencies that drive up expenses over time.

Quality control issues plague various procurement programs. The F-35 program, despite its massive cost, continues to experience technical difficulties. The Littoral Combat Ship program delivered vessels that failed to meet basic performance requirements while exceeding their budget. These challenges highlight the complexity of modern military procurement.

Recent global events have accelerated certain procurement priorities. The conflict in Ukraine prompted increased investment in precision weapons and air defense systems. Rising tensions in the Pacific drove naval procurement, particularly in amphibious warfare capabilities. These real-world demands shape procurement decisions and influence budget allocations.

The procurement budget reveals America's approach to military power: emphasizing technological superiority through advanced equipment, even at premium prices. This strategy delivers undeniable capabilities but raises questions about cost-effectiveness and sustainability as equipment prices continue to rise while competition among suppliers diminishes.

Building for War: $19B in Construction

At $19 billion, military construction represents the smallest major category in the defense budget, yet this figure finances a global building program that would dwarf most national construction efforts. This funding covers everything from new operational facilities to infrastructure upgrades, creating and maintaining the physical foundation of American military power worldwide.

The scope of military construction spans continents. In Japan alone, the military allocated $85 million for jet fuel tank facilities, enhancing force projection capabilities in the Pacific region. Another $75 million went toward a new operations support facility in Southern California. These projects, while appearing modest within the larger defense budget, prove crucial for maintaining global military readiness.

Military construction addresses immediate operational needs while anticipating future requirements. Bases require continuous upgrading to accommodate new weapons systems and changing strategic priorities. When the military acquires new aircraft, it often needs to modify hangars, reinforce runways, and construct specialized maintenance facilities. These adaptations consume significant portions of the construction budget.

Climate change has emerged as a major driver of military construction spending. The Department of Defense invests heavily in protecting bases from rising sea levels and extreme weather events. Guam's military installations, vital for America's Pacific presence, require extensive coastal infrastructure improvements to combat environmental threats. These climate-related adaptations represent an increasing share of construction expenses.

The military's construction program extends beyond traditional military facilities. The budget includes funding for schools on military bases, medical facilities for service members and their families, and housing infrastructure for personnel stationed worldwide. These support facilities prove essential for maintaining a professional, volunteer force with global responsibilities.

Infrastructure resilience commands increasing attention and resources. New facilities must withstand potential attacks while supporting critical operations. The military hardens key installations against missile strikes, particularly in the Pacific region, where growing tensions drive defensive construction priorities. These hardening efforts significantly increase building costs compared to civilian construction projects.

Base realignment and modernization efforts consume substantial construction resources. As strategic priorities shift and new technologies emerge, the military must modify or replace aging facilities. These projects often involve environmental remediation of old sites while developing new installations better suited to modern military requirements.

The construction budget also responds to evolving warfare concepts. Modern command centers require sophisticated communication infrastructure and cybersecurity provisions. Training facilities must accommodate increasingly complex weapons systems and simulation technologies. These specialized requirements drive construction costs well above civilian building standards.

Recent global developments have influenced construction priorities. The military has increased investment in Pacific region facilities, responding to growing strategic competition with China. European installations receive upgraded infrastructure to support NATO operations and regional deterrence efforts. These geographically focused construction programs reflect broader strategic priorities.

Quality of life considerations shape military construction decisions. New facilities must support service member morale while enabling efficient operations. The military builds fitness centers, recreational facilities, and modern housing units, recognizing that adequate infrastructure supports recruitment and retention efforts in an all-volunteer force.

Construction costs often exceed initial estimates due to unique military requirements. Security provisions, specialized materials, and remote locations drive expenses above comparable civilian projects. The military must also maintain higher building standards to ensure facilities remain operational under adverse conditions.

Energy efficiency and sustainability have become important factors in military construction. New facilities incorporate renewable energy systems and efficient design features, aiming to reduce long-term operating costs while enhancing energy security. These investments increase initial construction expenses but promise future operational savings.

The $19 billion construction budget, while modest compared to other military spending categories, plays a vital role in maintaining America's global military presence. Each project, from fuel tanks in Japan to training facilities in California, contributes to the military's ability to project power and respond to emerging threats worldwide.

USS Gerald R. Ford's $13.3B Price Tag

The USS Gerald R. Ford stands as the most expensive warship ever built, with a price tag of $13.3 billion. This single vessel - the first of a new class of supercarriers - costs more than many countries' entire military budgets and serves as a perfect case study of both American military ambition and procurement challenges.

The construction numbers alone tell a remarkable story. It took 49 million work hours to build the Ford - seven times the labor required to construct the Empire State Building. The vessel houses more than 750 bathrooms, each connected through a complex vacuum pressure system. When these systems malfunction, a single toilet repair can cost $400,000, requiring an acid flush with an unknown frequency of needed maintenance.

Initial planning for this massive vessel began in the 1990s. The Navy envisioned a new class of carrier that would lead the fleet for the next half century. Design began in earnest in the early 2000s, with projections estimating costs around $6.4 billion. But delays pushed the construction start from 2004 to 2005, then further. Each delay increased costs until the price reached $10 billion, before finally settling at $13.3 billion.

The Ford introduced nearly two dozen major new technologies, a decision that proved extremely costly. The most significant innovation was the electromagnetic aircraft launch system, replacing traditional steam-powered catapults. This system alone consumed over $1 billion in research and development costs, with installation costs more than doubling initial estimates. While promising fewer moving parts and improved reliability, the system faced significant technical challenges during development.

Advanced weapons elevators represent another technological challenge. The Ford features eleven such elevators, designed to move munitions more safely and efficiently than previous carriers. However, the last elevator wasn't certified operational until December 2021, years after the ship's commissioning. These delays significantly impacted the vessel's combat readiness while driving up costs.

The Ford's history illustrates common problems in military procurement. Despite accepting delivery in 2017, the Navy took possession before all systems were fully operational, hoping to stay under that year's budget requirements. Four years later, the carrier was still undergoing final tests before its first full deployment. The rush to deploy new technology without adequate testing led to costly modifications and delays.

Maintenance costs for the Ford class present another sobering reality. The ship's complex systems require specialized maintenance, often demanding contractor support rather than traditional Navy personnel. This ongoing dependency on private contractors for basic operations adds significantly to the vessel's lifetime costs.

The Ford also needs modification to accommodate the F-35 fighter jet, despite being America's newest carrier. This retrofit will cost an additional $315 million - an expense that could have been avoided with better program integration. The next carrier in the class incorporates these modifications during construction, but at additional expense.

Perhaps most concerning, the ship failed to achieve level one survivability - the ability to continue operations after an underwater explosive attack. This shortcoming emerged in 2010, the same year the Navy pushed Congress to approve contracts for additional carriers of the same class.

The Ford's story reveals how modern military procurement often prioritizes technological advancement over cost control or practical considerations. The decision to incorporate so many new technologies simultaneously - against standard procurement wisdom - created cascading delays and cost overruns that could have been avoided with a more measured approach.

Yet despite these issues, the Navy continues building Ford-class carriers, with each ship costing billions in construction and requiring decades of expensive maintenance. These massive investments reflect America's commitment to maintaining naval supremacy, regardless of cost.

The USS Gerald R. Ford serves as more than just a warship - it represents both the ambitions and challenges of modern military procurement. Its $13.3 billion price tag raises crucial questions about military spending priorities and the balance between technological advancement and fiscal responsibility.

Chapter Three

Global Military Presence

The Network: 1,250 Military Bases

The United States maintains approximately 1,250 military bases worldwide, a network so vast it surpasses any empire in history. Of these installations, about 800 exist outside American territory, spread across 80 different countries. This unprecedented global presence forms the backbone of American military power projection, costing roughly $55 billion annually just to maintain.

These bases range from massive installations that function as small American cities to shared outposts with host nation forces. Each serves a strategic purpose in America's global military posture. Unlike historical empires that built bases through conquest, the United States has established most of these facilities through cooperation with host nations, creating a web of military partnerships unprecedented in scale.

The U.S. military transforms these bases into small pieces of America abroad. They feature American restaurant chains like Pizza Hut, McDonald's, and Subway. Commissaries stock American products flown in from the United States, ensuring service members have access to familiar foods and products. This commitment to recreating American life overseas comes at significant cost but is deemed essential for maintaining morale among deployed personnel.

This base network serves multiple functions beyond combat operations. Many installations act as strategic deterrents, positioned near potential adversaries. Others serve as logistics hubs, enabling rapid response to regional crises. The bases also facilitate humanitarian operations, disaster relief, and military training with allied forces.

The financial implications of maintaining this global presence are substantial. Beyond the $55 billion in direct maintenance costs, each base requires extensive support infrastructure. The military must maintain supply lines, provide medical services, operate schools for service members' children, and manage utilities in locations ranging from desert outposts to tropical islands.

Host nations often share costs for these installations, recognizing their mutual security benefits. In many cases, these bases enhance the host nation's own military capabilities through training opportunities and shared resources. However, the bulk of operational and maintenance expenses falls to the American taxpayer.

The bases also serve as platforms for power projection. Aircraft carriers may grab headlines, but these fixed installations provide the permanent infrastructure needed to support global operations. They house fuel reserves, ammunition stockpiles, repair facilities, and the countless other resources required to sustain military operations far from American shores.

Each base represents a long-term investment in regional security. When the military establishes a new installation, it commits to decades of infrastructure development and maintenance. This creates both strategic advantages and financial obligations that extend far into the future.

The network's composition continues to evolve with changing strategic priorities. Recent years have seen increased focus on Pacific region facilities, responding to China's growing military capabilities. European bases have gained renewed importance amid tensions with Russia. Each adjustment to this global posture carries significant costs in infrastructure modifications and support requirements.

Critics argue this vast network of bases represents unnecessary military overreach and wasteful spending. Supporters counter that these installations form the foundation of American global influence, enabling rapid response to crises while deterring potential adversaries. The reality likely lies between these viewpoints, as each base serves specific strategic purposes while contributing to overall maintenance costs.

What's clear is that this network of 1,250 bases represents a unique approach to global military presence. No other nation maintains anything approaching this scale of overseas installations. The network embodies America's commitment to global military engagement, but it also locks in long-term spending requirements that contribute significantly to overall defense costs.

800 Bases Beyond American Shores

Of the United States' 1,250 military installations, approximately 800 exist outside American territory, creating an unprecedented network of foreign bases that spans 80 nations. These overseas installations form a critical component of America's global military strategy, enabling the U.S. to maintain what the Pentagon calls "global reach" - the ability to respond to threats or crises anywhere in the world.

The scale of these foreign bases reflects America's unique military posture. Unlike other major powers that focus primarily on regional influence, the United States has transformed the entire world into its operating environment. Each foreign base serves as a forward position, allowing the military to maintain constant presence in strategic regions worldwide.

These installations aren't sparse outposts - they're fully functioning American communities. The military has effectively created "Little Americas" in foreign countries, complete with familiar comforts from home. The bases feature American restaurant chains, grocery stores stocked with U.S. products, and comprehensive support facilities for service members and their families.

The financial commitment to these overseas bases is substantial. The military must transport American products worldwide to stock base facilities. Each installation requires extensive infrastructure - housing, medical facilities, schools for military children, maintenance facilities, and recreational areas. Simply maintaining this global network costs approximately $55 billion annually.

Host nations often share these bases' costs and welcome their presence. In the Philippines, for example, the government actively sought increased U.S. military presence for regional security. Many installations enhance host nation military capabilities through joint training and shared resources. However, the majority of operational costs fall to American taxpayers.

These foreign bases serve multiple functions beyond military operations. They act as staging areas for humanitarian missions, support disaster relief efforts, and enable rapid response to regional crises. The bases also facilitate military cooperation with allied nations, strengthening diplomatic relationships through joint exercises and training programs.

The strategic placement of these bases reflects America's global security concerns. Installations near China support Pacific deterrence efforts. European bases strengthen NATO operations. Middle Eastern facilities enable rapid response to regional conflicts while ensuring the free flow of oil through vital shipping lanes.

Maintaining this overseas presence requires complex logistics. The military must coordinate supply chains spanning continents, manage international agreements with host nations, and ensure consistent operational standards across diverse geographic and cultural environments. This complexity contributes significantly to the Department of Defense's operating costs.

Recent global developments have highlighted these bases' strategic importance. The conflict in Ukraine demonstrated the value of European installations in supporting allied nations. Rising tensions in the Pacific have emphasized the significance of bases near potential flashpoints. Each crisis reinforces the role these facilities play in American military strategy.

This network of 800 foreign bases represents more than military infrastructure - it embodies America's approach to global security. Through these installations, the United States maintains constant presence in strategic regions, enabling rapid response to threats while demonstrating commitment to allies and partners worldwide.

Slices of America Abroad

The U.S. military has created something unprecedented at its overseas bases - miniature versions of American life transplanted onto foreign soil. These installations aren't just military outposts; they're fully functioning American communities where service members can find familiar comforts from home, from fast food to grocery stores stocked with American products.

On these bases, service members can walk into a Pizza Hut, order from McDonald's, or grab a sandwich at Subway - all while stationed thousands of miles from American shores. The commissaries stock products flown directly from the United States, ensuring military personnel have access to familiar brands and foods. This commitment to recreating American life abroad comes at significant cost, but military planners consider it essential for maintaining morale among deployed personnel.

The infrastructure at these bases extends far beyond dining options. The military constructs comprehensive support facilities including American-style housing, schools for service members' children, medical facilities, and recreation centers. These amenities create environments where military families can maintain a semblance of normal American life while serving overseas.

Support services at these installations mirror those found in any American community. The bases employ teachers for military schools, maintain medical staff for base hospitals, and provide various family support services. Each base essentially operates as a self-contained American town, requiring substantial resources to maintain this level of infrastructure abroad.

The military's dedication to creating these "Little Americas" speaks to a broader strategy of maintaining a professional, volunteer force capable of long-term overseas deployments. By providing familiar comforts and comprehensive support services, the military aims to make foreign deployments more sustainable for service members and their families.

Transportation logistics for maintaining these American environments overseas consume significant resources. The military must coordinate regular shipments of American products, manage complex supply chains, and ensure consistent availability of everything from food items to maintenance supplies. This logistical effort represents a substantial portion of the military's operational costs.

These facilities serve purposes beyond troop comfort. They function as showcases of American culture and lifestyle in host nations. The bases often employ local civilians, creating economic ties with surrounding communities. They also serve as platforms for cultural exchange, though this integration remains limited by security requirements.

The cost of maintaining these American environments overseas contributes to the larger expenses of global military presence. Flying American products to bases worldwide, maintaining American-standard facilities, and providing comprehensive support services all add to the military's operational budget. However, military leadership views these expenses as necessary investments in force readiness and morale.

The Cost of Global Coverage

The financial reality of maintaining America's global military presence is staggering. The U.S. military spends $55 billion annually just to keep its worldwide network of bases operational. This figure represents more than the entire military budgets of most nations, yet it covers only the basic maintenance and operational costs of American installations worldwide.

Basic operational expenses consume enormous resources. Just moving an Armored Brigade Combat Team one mile costs $66,000 in fuel and maintenance. Multiply this across global operations, training exercises, and regular rotations of forces, and transportation costs alone reach astronomical levels. The military must maintain a fleet of over 800 transport aircraft and 450 aerial refueling tankers just to support this global movement of personnel and equipment.

Infrastructure costs create another major expense category. Every foreign base requires continuous investment in facilities maintenance, from runway repairs to housing upkeep. The military spent $85 million for jet fuel tanks in Japan and $75 million for a single operational support facility in Southern California. These individual projects multiply across hundreds of installations worldwide.

Personnel costs increase significantly with global deployment. Service members stationed overseas receive additional allowances and benefits. The military must provide housing, healthcare, education for dependents, and various support services at each location. Creating and maintaining these support systems at hundreds of installations worldwide requires substantial ongoing investment.

Supply chain logistics for global operations generate massive expenses. The military must transport everything from ammunition to groceries to bases worldwide. Each installation requires regular resupply of fuel, spare parts, food, and countless other necessities. The complexity of managing these global supply chains adds significant costs to basic operational expenses.

Environmental challenges add another layer of expenses. The military must invest in protecting bases from climate change impacts, particularly in coastal areas. Facilities in Guam, for example, require extensive infrastructure improvements to combat rising sea levels. These environmental adaptations represent growing costs in maintaining global military presence.

Healthcare infrastructure spans the globe, with the military maintaining medical facilities at major installations worldwide. The $39 billion spent annually on military healthcare must cover services wherever American forces deploy. This global medical network requires specialized equipment, trained personnel, and regular supply chain support.

Security requirements at overseas bases drive additional costs. Each installation needs defensive capabilities, surveillance systems, and security personnel. The military must also harden facilities against potential threats, particularly in strategic locations near potential adversaries. These security measures significantly increase basic operational costs.

Communications infrastructure represents another major expense. The military maintains complex networks linking installations worldwide, requiring satellite systems, secure communications equipment, and dedicated personnel. This global communications backbone enables command and control but demands substantial investment to maintain and secure.

Training exercises with allied nations, while strategically valuable, add to operational costs. The military conducts regular joint exercises worldwide, requiring transportation of personnel and equipment, plus additional logistical support. These activities strengthen military partnerships but contribute significantly to overall operational expenses.

The cost of global coverage extends beyond direct military expenses. The U.S. provides substantial security assistance to host nations, funds infrastructure improvements in partner countries, and maintains diplomatic support structures worldwide. These auxiliary costs, while often overlooked, form an integral part of maintaining global military presence.

Strategic Positioning and Power Projection

America's approach to global military presence represents something unprecedented in history. Unlike traditional empires that secured territories through conquest, the United States has built a network of bases through strategic partnerships, allowing it to project power across every corner of the globe. This system enables the U.S. to enforce rules and maintain order in a world system it helped create and from which it benefits immensely.

The military's strategic positioning follows clear patterns. To counter China, considered a major rival, the U.S. has established bases in smaller neighboring countries. Naval bases dot the Pacific, enabling rapid response to regional tensions. European installations support NATO operations and provide deterrence against Russian aggression. Middle Eastern bases ensure the free flow of oil - not primarily for U.S. benefit, as America imports most of its oil from Canada, but to maintain global economic stability.

Power projection capabilities rest heavily on naval forces. The U.S. Navy patrols global maritime shipping routes through which, according to United Nations data, approximately 80% of world trade by volume and 70% by value travels. This naval presence helps secure international commerce, contributing to global economic stability while demonstrating American military reach.

Aircraft carriers serve as mobile bases, providing flexible power projection capabilities worldwide. The Navy maintains four consecutive carrier deployments across the globe at any given time, each deployment costing upwards of $46 million annually. These floating airports can deliver troops, vehicles, electronic warfare capabilities, and air defense assets to any coastline on Earth.

In the Pacific region alone, the U.S. has allocated $6.1 billion for supporting operations. This includes $1.8 billion for modernizing facilities and equipment, and $2.3 billion for training exercises, experimentation, and innovation. Another $1.2 billion goes toward improving infrastructure resilience, particularly against air and missile attacks and climate change impacts.

European operations receive $4.2 billion in funding, reflecting renewed strategic focus in the region. This includes support for approximately 200 additional personnel managing logistics for equipment supporting Ukraine operations. The military maintains prepositioned equipment throughout Europe, enabling rapid response to potential crises.

The Middle East, despite reduced tensions, still commands significant resources. While Central Command's budget decreased from $34.3 billion to $27.3 billion, substantial investments continue in force protection ($5.6 billion) and in-theater support ($16.9 billion). These expenditures maintain America's ability to respond to regional developments and protect vital interests.

Strategic positioning extends beyond combat capabilities. The military maintains disaster response resources worldwide, enabling humanitarian operations wherever needed. This capability demonstrates American power through assistance rather than force, supporting diplomatic objectives while maintaining operational presence in strategic regions.

Modern power projection increasingly relies on advanced technology. The military positions missile defense systems, surveillance capabilities, and communication networks globally. These systems enable rapid response to threats while demonstrating technological superiority - a key component of American military deterrence.

This global positioning strategy reflects America's unique approach to military power: maintaining constant presence, demonstrating capabilities through regular operations, and combining hard and soft power to achieve strategic objectives. The cost proves substantial, but military planners consider it essential for maintaining global stability and protecting American interests worldwide.

Chapter Four

The Technology of War

The F-35 Program: $35,000 Per Flight Hour

The F-35 Lightning II program stands as the most expensive weapons system in military history, with total costs projected to reach $1.7 trillion. Currently, the U.S. military operates 630 of these aircraft, with plans to acquire 2,000 more. But the real story isn't just in the acquisition costs - it's in the staggering $35,000 price tag for every hour these software aircraft spend in the air.

After sixteen years since its first flight, the F-35 continues to face over 600 documented problems, primarily related to computer and hardware issues. Despite these challenges, the military continues procurement because the aircraft represents the future of aerial warfare. The program includes three distinct variants designed for different military branches: the F-35A for the Air Force at $78 million each, the F-35B for the Marine Corps at $101 million, and the F-35C for the Navy at $94 million.

Maintenance costs for the F-35 fleet have spiraled beyond initial projections. Between 2018 and 2021, lifetime maintenance cost estimates increased by 15%, reaching over $400 billion. By comparison, operating an older F-16 costs approximately $22,000 per hour, highlighting the significant cost increase for maintaining these advanced aircraft.

The program's complexity extends to pilot equipment. Each F-35 pilot requires a custom-fitted helmet costing $400,000. These helmets combine traditional heads-up display capabilities with night vision and feeds from infrared cameras mounted on the aircraft's body. The precision required for these systems demands perfect alignment to prevent pilots from experiencing double vision.

Despite its problems, pilots praise the F-35's capabilities. The aircraft's stealth design, advanced sensors, and data fusion systems provide unprecedented battlefield awareness. Pilots can detect and engage targets before being detected themselves, a capability that advocates argue justifies the program's enormous costs.

The maintenance challenges stem partly from the aircraft's sophisticated computer systems. The F-35 contains 8 million lines of code for basic operations, plus another 16 million lines for diagnostic tools. While this complexity enables advanced capabilities, it also creates substantial maintenance requirements and potential points of failure.

Training pilots for the F-35 represents another significant cost center. The Air Force spends approximately $10.7 million to train each F-35 pilot. These costs reflect both the aircraft's complexity and the military's commitment to ensuring pilots can fully utilize its advanced capabilities.

The program's massive scale impacts America's allies as well. Beyond U.S. purchases, Lockheed Martin has delivered over 200 F-35s to partner nations, with orders for 600 more in process. This international participation helps offset development costs but also creates global dependencies on American military technology.

Low-rate initial production continues as the Pentagon has delayed full-rate production authorization. This decision reflects ongoing concerns about unresolved technical issues and the need to ensure the aircraft meets all performance requirements before committing to maximum production rates.

Modern Weapons and Their Costs

The raw numbers tell a startling story of modern military technology's costs. A single cruise missile costs $1.6 million, and in 2023 alone, the military purchased 600 of them. Each helicopter requires $21 million, while basic combat vehicles command $372,000 apiece. These prices reflect not just the sophistication of modern warfare but also the complex system that produces these weapons.

The cruise missile program exemplifies modern weapon costs. The military spent $1.6 million for each missile, then ordered them by the hundreds. The Patriot missile system development required $1.037 billion for 252 missiles and their launch platforms. The GMLRS (Guided Multiple Launch Rocket System) program consumed $812 million to acquire 4,718 rockets, primarily replacing those provided to Ukraine.

Helicopter procurement reveals similar cost patterns. The CH-53K King Stallion program received $2.3 billion for just ten aircraft. These represent the world's most powerful heavy-lift helicopters, capable of delivering supplies, equipment, and artillery pieces during amphibious operations. The military also allocated $1.2 billion for 56 Black Hawk helicopters, essential for troop transport and combat support missions.

Combat vehicle costs demonstrate how even basic military equipment carries substantial price tags. The military purchased 3,700 troop transport vehicles at $372,000 each in one year, following up with an order for 3,100 more the following year. These vehicles, designed to move troops around the battlefield, require sophisticated armor and electronics that drive up their cost.

The procurement pattern usually involves large-scale purchases. For naval forces, the military spent $7.3 billion on two Virginia-class submarines and $5.6 billion on two Arleigh Burke destroyers. Even support vessels command significant prices, with two fleet replenishment oilers costing $1 billion and a single towing and rescue ship requiring $100 million.

Price inflation in weapons systems has become a serious concern. The Stinger missile that once cost $25,000 now approaches half a million dollars, far exceeding normal inflation rates. This pattern repeats across multiple weapons systems, driven by limited competition among contractors and increasingly complex technical requirements.

The military also invests heavily in unmanned systems. Nearly $3 billion went to various drone programs, including the Triton, Stingray, and Reaper platforms. A specialized program received $200 million to develop stealthy drones for special operations forces, combining long loiter times with precise strike capabilities.

Next-Generation Military Systems

The U.S. military's research and development programs are creating weapons that seem drawn from science fiction. The Pentagon invests heavily in laser weapons for ships, autonomous submarines that can operate independently, and exoskeletons designed to give soldiers superhuman strength. These next-generation systems consume $140 billion annually in research and development funding - equivalent to Morocco's entire economy.

Artificial intelligence stands at the forefront of military innovation. The Pentagon channels significant resources into AI systems that analyze drone footage, enhance targeting capabilities, and develop autonomous combat platforms. This investment extends beyond basic research, with the military spending $28 million in one year just to hire artificial intelligence experts.

Naval warfare is undergoing revolutionary changes with new technology. The military has allocated $300 million for large unmanned surface vessels, exploring how robotic ships might counter China's growing naval fleet. While still in development, these autonomous vessels represent the Navy's effort to offset numerical disadvantages through technological superiority.

The Space Based Missile Warning System, receiving $4.7 billion in funding, represents another leap forward in military technology. This network of advanced satellites will replace aging early warning systems, providing faster threat identification and response capabilities. The program includes $1.8 billion for a new generation of GPS satellites with enhanced anti-jamming capabilities.

The Army's Precision Strike Missile program demonstrates the evolution of conventional weapons. These next-generation missiles, replacing the older ATACMS system, recently debuted in Ukraine to significant effect. The military has ordered 120 of these advanced missiles for continued testing and evaluation.

The push for technological superiority extends to basic combat equipment. The military leads worldwide development in advanced thermal optics, body armor, and small arms. Even support systems receive significant upgrades, with new logistics capabilities and training facilities incorporating cutting-edge technology.

Cyber capabilities represent another crucial development area. The military invests heavily in cyber warfare systems, recognizing future conflicts will involve digital battlegrounds as much as physical ones. These investments cover both offensive capabilities and defensive systems protecting military networks.

The development of these advanced systems reflects America's approach to warfare: maintaining overwhelming technological advantages to deter potential adversaries while reducing risks to U.S. personnel. However, this strategy comes with significant costs, both in development and eventual deployment of these sophisticated weapons.

From Military Labs to Civilian Life

The U.S. military's $140 billion research and development budget produces more than just weapons systems. Many technologies we use daily originated in military laboratories. The internet itself was created for and by the Department of Defense. GPS navigation, voice recognition, computer mice, and drone technology - all emerged from military research before transforming civilian life.

The military's research investment follows both immediate combat needs and long-term technological breakthroughs. While some projects focus on battlefield advantages, others yield unexpected civilian benefits. Military research into artificial intelligence, initially aimed at analyzing drone footage and improving targeting capabilities, has contributed to civilian AI applications.

Basic research in material sciences, funded through military programs, often finds civilian applications. The Pentagon's investment in communications technology has repeatedly revolutionized how the world connects. The military's early development of the internet began as a secure communication network before becoming the foundation of modern digital life.

Healthcare advances frequently emerge from military research. The Pentagon invests $1.5 billion annually in medical research, developing new treatments initially intended for combat injuries. These innovations often transfer to civilian medical practice, improving care for the general population.

Transportation technology demonstrates another area where military research benefits civilian life. The development of advanced navigation systems, initially for military purposes, now guides civilian vehicles worldwide. Even commercial aviation benefits from military research into safety systems and flight technology.

The military's focus on autonomous systems extends beyond combat applications. Research into self-driving vehicles, while primarily targeting military logistics, contributes to civilian autonomous vehicle development. Drone technology, first developed for military surveillance, now serves numerous civilian purposes from photography to package delivery.

This technology transfer from military to civilian applications represents an often-overlooked benefit of defense spending. While the primary goal remains military capability, the spillover effects continue to shape civilian technology and innovation.

Chapter Five

The Defense Industry Reality

The Big Five Contractors.

The reality of American military spending cannot be understood without examining the handful of companies that dominate the defense industry. What was once a diverse field of 51 defense contractors has consolidated into just five major players: Lockheed Martin, Raytheon, Boeing, Northrop Grumman, and General Dynamics. These corporations receive 466 billion dollars - approximately 54% of the entire defense budget - creating what amounts to a monopoly over American military production.

Lockheed Martin stands as perhaps the most prominent example of this concentrated power. The company receives more money from the U.S. government annually - $47.5 billion - than NASA's entire budget. If Lockheed Martin were a federal agency, it would rank as the 24th largest, receiving more government funding than the majority of actual government departments. Through this massive funding, the corporation generates nearly a billion dollars in profit every month.

The concentration of power among these five contractors has fundamentally altered the dynamics of military procurement. When the Pentagon needs a new weapons system, it often faces a single bidder. The F-35 fighter program illustrates this problem perfectly. Boeing's decision to withdraw from the competition in 2019 left Northrop Grumman as the sole bidder, essentially allowing the company to name its price.

These contractors' influence extends far beyond mere production. The Department of Defense has become, in their own words, "increasingly reliant on a small number of contractors for critical defense capabilities." This dependency creates a situation where these companies become "too important to fail." The military cannot afford to let them go bankrupt because they're the only ones capable of producing vital military technologies.

The financial implications of this consolidated power are staggering. The companies can charge essentially whatever they want for their products, knowing the

Pentagon has nowhere else to go. A stinger missile that once cost $25,000 now commands nearly half a million dollars - a price increase that far outstrips inflation. The military pays Boeing $3,357 for a ball bearing that costs $15 in the Pentagon's own warehouse.

These contractors have also mastered the art of political influence. In 2023, Lockheed Martin spent $2.7 million on political contributions, split evenly between Democrats and Republicans. This represents just one company's spending in a single election cycle, with the amount expected to increase as elections approach. The goal is simple: cultivate relationships with lawmakers who control defense spending.

The revolving door between these contractors and the Pentagon further cements their influence. In 2022 alone, top defense companies hired 672 former Pentagon employees as lobbyists, board members, and executives. This creates a system where government officials who control contract awards know they can secure lucrative private sector positions with the very companies they oversee.

The geographical strategy of these contractors proves particularly effective. They strategically locate facilities across congressional districts, ensuring that cuts to military spending would mean job losses in multiple political jurisdictions. This makes reducing military spending politically difficult, as no representative wants to be responsible for unemployment in their district.

The result is a self-perpetuating system where these five companies maintain their dominance through political influence, strategic hiring, and careful manipulation of economic dependencies. They've created an environment where reducing military spending becomes nearly impossible, despite clear evidence of overcharging and waste.

The contractors justify their prices through claims of complexity and advanced technology. However, investigations repeatedly reveal profit margins of 40-50%, far exceeding what would be considered reasonable in a truly competitive market. These excessive profits come directly from taxpayer dollars, with little effective oversight or control.

This concentration of power among five contractors represents a fundamental shift from historical patterns of military procurement. During World War II, numerous companies converted their civilian production to support the war effort. Today, these specialized defense contractors maintain effective monopolies over military production, limiting competition and driving up costs across the entire defense sector.

From 51 to 5: The Consolidation Story

The transformation of America's defense industry from 51 independent contractors to just five dominant corporations represents one of the most significant consolidations of industrial power in history. In the Pentagon's own words, the defense industry underwent a dramatic "transitioning from 51 to five aerospace and defense prime contractors." This consolidation has fundamentally altered how America equips its military and manages its defense spending.

The story begins in the aftermath of World War II, when numerous companies contributed to the military industrial base. During the war, America's manufacturing might proved decisive, with companies from automakers to electronics manufacturers converting their production to support the war effort. In the six years leading to the war, the U.S. built 20,000 aircraft. During the conflict, American manufacturers produced an astounding 300,000 aircraft.

The Cold War era maintained this diverse industrial base. Companies like McDonald Douglas, Hughes, Grumman, Northrop, and many others competed for military contracts. This competition drove innovation while helping control costs. During this period, numerous aerospace and defense companies operated independently, each specializing in different aspects of military production.

The end of the Cold War marked a turning point. With reduced military spending anticipated, the Department of Defense warned contractors of massive cutbacks. This triggered what the transcripts describe as a "feeding frenzy of consolidation and acquisition" as companies prepared for what they believed would be the first sustained period of peace in their existence.

However, the consolidation created an unexpected problem. As smaller companies were absorbed by larger ones, the Pentagon found itself increasingly dependent on a shrinking number of contractors for critical defense capabilities. This dependency has reached the point where the military can't afford to let any of the remaining five major contractors fail - they've become essential to national security.

The consolidation's impact becomes clear in modern procurement. When the Pentagon needs new equipment, it often faces a single bidder. The Sentinel missile program, meant to replace aging Minuteman III ICBMs, demonstrates this problem. The program, already costing $96 billion, faces delays and cost overruns partly because there's no competitive pressure to control costs.

This consolidation has created what amounts to regional monopolies in military production. Each of the five major contractors - Lockheed Martin, Raytheon, Boeing, Northrop Grumman, and General Dynamics - dominates particular aspects of defense production. If the Pentagon needs an F-35, it must work with Lockheed Martin. There are no alternatives.

The result is a procurement system where competition barely exists. The Pentagon reports that two-thirds of major weapons system contracts receive bids from just one company. Some contracts are awarded without any competitive bidding process, simply because no other company can produce the required equipment.

This lack of competition directly impacts military spending. When the Pentagon has nowhere else to go for essential equipment, contractors can essentially name their price. The result is cost increases that far exceed inflation, with some components costing many times more than identical items available elsewhere.

The consolidation's effects extend beyond mere pricing. These five companies now control vast amounts of technical knowledge and manufacturing capability. They employ thousands of skilled workers and maintain specialized facilities that would be difficult or impossible to replicate. This creates a form of institutional knowledge monopoly, further cementing their position in the defense industry.

Monopoly and Price Inflation

The consequences of having only five major defense contractors become starkly clear when examining military equipment prices. The Pentagon faces a troubling reality: with no real competition in the defense market, contractors can charge virtually any price they want. The result is a pattern of price inflation that defies normal market logic and strains the military budget.

The Stinger missile offers a perfect example of this unchecked price inflation. What once cost the Pentagon $25,000 now commands nearly half a million dollars for the same missile. This price increase - more than 16 times the original cost - far exceeds any reasonable inflation rate. With no alternative suppliers, the military must pay whatever price contractors demand for these essential weapons.

Perhaps the most egregious example of price inflation comes from Boeing. A Pentagon inspector discovered the military paying Boeing $3,357 for a single ball bearing - a part available in the Pentagon's own warehouse for just $15.42. This markup of more than 21,000 percent demonstrates how monopolistic control allows contractors to charge extraordinary prices for even the simplest components.

The problem extends across all types of military equipment. When contractors investigate their own pricing, they often find profit margins of 40 to 50 percent - far above what would be possible in a competitive market. These excessive profits come directly from taxpayer dollars, with contractors earning hundreds of millions more than they would in a normal business environment.

The dining facilities at military bases illustrate how this price inflation affects even basic services. One contractor, KBR, was found to be overcharging by 30 to 40 percent for dining hall operations. This pattern of overcharging extends from complex weapons systems down to fundamental support services.

The F-35 program demonstrates how monopolistic control affects major weapons systems. Each hour of flight costs $35,000 - significantly more than the older F-16's operating cost of $22,000 per hour. With no alternative fighter program available, the military must accept these increased operational costs.

The problem compounds because many contracts are awarded without competitive bidding. The Department of Defense reports that two-thirds of major weapons systems contracts receive bids from only one company. Some contracts are awarded without any bidding process, simply because only one company can produce the required equipment.

The monopolistic nature of defense contracting creates a self-perpetuating cycle. As prices rise, more money flows to contractors, who then use their increased profits to strengthen their market position through political influence and strategic acquisitions. This further reduces competition and enables even higher prices.

The Inspector General of the Department of Defense has repeatedly found evidence of overcharging through corruption, waste, and fraud. Despite these findings, the fundamental structure of the defense industry makes meaningful reform difficult. The military's dependence on these five contractors limits its ability to demand reasonable prices.

This price inflation affects military readiness. Every overpriced component means fewer resources available for other needs. When basic parts cost hundreds or thousands of times their actual value, the military must either reduce quantities purchased or seek additional funding from Congress.

The $15 vs. $3,357 Reality

The story of a single ball bearing exposes everything wrong with America's military procurement system. When a Pentagon inspector investigated military purchasing, they discovered something astonishing: Boeing was charging the military $3,357 for a basic ball bearing that cost just $15.42 in the Pentagon's own warehouse. This 21,000% markup serves as a perfect case study of how defense contractors exploit their monopolistic position.

This price disparity wasn't an isolated incident. The same pattern repeats across thousands of components and systems. The Stinger missile, once purchased for $25,000, now costs nearly half a million dollars - with no significant improvements or upgrades to justify the price increase. When questioned about such markups, contractors often cite complexity, security requirements, or specialized manufacturing needs. Yet the ball bearing case strips away these excuses, revealing pure price gouging.

The implications reach far beyond a single overpriced part. The military buys thousands of components, and similar markups occur throughout the system. The Pentagon's own investigations reveal contractors routinely taking profit margins of 40-50% - far above what would be possible in a competitive market. These excessive profits come directly from taxpayer dollars, with contractors earning hundreds of millions more than justified by their actual costs.

KBR's dining facility operations provide another clear example. The contractor overcharged by 30-40% for basic food services at military bases. Even fundamental support services face massive markups when filtered through the defense contracting system. The problem extends from the smallest components to the largest weapons systems.

The root cause becomes clear when examining the procurement process. With only five major defense contractors remaining, the Pentagon often has nowhere else to go for essential equipment and services. Two-thirds of major weapons systems contracts receive bids from just one company. Some contracts are awarded without any competitive bidding process because only one contractor can provide the required items.

This reality creates a perverse incentive structure. Contractors know the military must maintain certain capabilities, and with no alternative suppliers, they can essentially name their price. The ball bearing example shows how this plays out - even when identical parts are available at normal market prices, the military often must pay whatever contractors demand.

The situation grows worse because many lawmakers who oversee military spending own stock in these same defense companies. The contractors spend millions on political contributions and employ hundreds of former

Pentagon officials. This creates a system where those responsible for controlling costs have financial incentives to allow overcharging.

The $15 versus $3,357 reality reveals a fundamental breakdown in military procurement. When a basic part can cost 200 times its actual value, the entire system needs scrutiny. Yet reform proves difficult because these same contractors have become "too important to fail" - the military depends on them for critical capabilities and can't risk their financial collapse.

Failed Audits and Missing Assets

The Pentagon faces a startling accountability crisis: after six consecutive years of attempting independent audits, it has failed every single time. Even more alarming, 61% of the military's physical assets are effectively missing - they can't be located or accounted for in any tracking system. This means the Department of Defense, with its $916 billion budget, cannot reliably track more than half of everything it owns.

The scale of this accounting failure is unprecedented in federal government. While other departments routinely pass their audits, the Pentagon remains the only federal agency unable to account for its spending and assets. Even creating the report to track military expenditures costs $269,000, yet the resulting document fails to provide clear accountability for hundreds of billions in spending.

This lack of oversight leads to wasteful spending patterns. The military likely purchases equipment it already owns simply because it can't locate existing inventory. When accountants attempt to track these assets, they face an insurmountable task - the Pentagon's financial systems are so complex and disconnected that even professional auditors throw up their hands in defeat.

The problem extends beyond mere bookkeeping. American taxpayers want to know how their money is being spent, especially given that military spending consumes nearly half of all discretionary federal spending. The fact that the department receiving such a huge portion of the federal budget cannot account for its expenditures represents a serious concern for public accountability.

The missing assets highlight deeper systematic problems. The military might own perfectly good equipment but purchase replacements because tracking systems can't locate original items. This creates a cycle of redundant purchasing that benefits contractors while wasting taxpayer money. The lack of accurate inventory tracking makes it impossible to determine whether new purchases are truly necessary.

These failed audits reveal how the consolidation of defense contractors compounds accountability problems. With only five major contractors controlling most military production, there's little incentive to maintain transparent pricing or efficient inventory management. The system's complexity serves contractor interests by making it harder to track costs and identify overcharging.

The situation grows more concerning because despite these accountability failures, military spending continues to increase. Without accurate tracking of existing assets and expenditures, the Pentagon cannot effectively evaluate whether additional spending truly serves military needs or simply adds to an already unmanageable inventory system.

Chapter Six

The Political Machine

The Revolving Door System

The military-industrial complex operates on a system so blatant it's earned its own metaphor: the revolving door. While not a physical door, this continuous cycle of personnel moving between the Pentagon and defense contractors represents one of the most powerful forces driving military spending. The numbers tell a striking story: in 2022 alone, top defense companies hired 672 employees directly from the Pentagon to serve as lobbyists, board members, and executives.

The case of Jim Mattis perfectly illustrates this revolving door in action. After serving decades in the military and retiring as a general, Mattis joined the board of General Dynamics, a major defense contractor. He then passed through the metaphorical door again to become Secretary of Defense under President Trump. After his government service, Mattis returned to General Dynamics' board, bringing with him invaluable insider knowledge, government contacts, and influence accumulated during his time at the Pentagon.

This isn't an isolated case - it's standard practice in Washington. The revolving door spins so frequently that defense contractors have established their offices in an area literally called "Pentagon City," just steps away from the military headquarters they service. This physical proximity mirrors the close relationship between the military and its contractors.

The mechanics of this system are straightforward but effective. When someone works in government deciding on contracts, they often have conversations with potential contractors. These companies can promise lucrative post-government positions, creating an incentive for officials to award generous contracts to their future employers. This "quid pro quo" arrangement ensures officials receive high-paying jobs after leaving government service.

The impact of this revolving door extends beyond individual careers. Former Pentagon officials bring insider knowledge about military needs, budgeting processes, and decision-making procedures to their new corporate roles. This information proves invaluable for contractors seeking to secure lucrative military contracts, effectively giving them an inside track on billions in government spending.

Geography reinforces these connections. The Pentagon and major defense contractors cluster together in Northern Virginia, creating an ecosystem where personal and professional relationships blur. This proximity facilitates the constant movement of personnel between public and private sectors, making the revolving door not just metaphorical but physical.

The consequences of this system are profound. When defense contractors hire former military officials, they gain more than just employees - they acquire influence within the Pentagon's decision-making process. These former officials understand how to navigate military bureaucracy and know which buttons to push to secure contracts and funding.

The revolving door also affects military planning and procurement decisions. Officials who anticipate future employment with contractors may favor expensive, contractor-friendly solutions over more cost-effective alternatives. This creates a bias toward higher spending that serves contractor interests rather than military needs or taxpayer concerns.

Jobs, Votes, and Military Spending

Defense contractors have mastered a powerful political strategy: strategically placing their operations across congressional districts to make military spending cuts politically impossible. An Air Force veteran and analyst named Christian Sorensen mapped this deliberate distribution of defense facilities, revealing how contractors create jobs across dozens of states and political districts to ensure continued political support.

The system works with ruthless efficiency. When lawmakers consider reducing military spending, they face an immediate political threat: job losses in their districts. No representative wants to be known as the politician who caused local unemployment. As one expert noted, "No Congress person wants to be the person who loses jobs in their district. Nobody wants to be the one known as shutting down a plant and people becoming unemployed."

Senator Roger Wicker of Mississippi exemplifies this dynamic perfectly. As a member of the U.S. Senate Committee on Armed Services, he plays a crucial role in approving military spending. His state hosts a massive naval shipyard run by defense contractor Huntington Ingalls - the largest employer in Mississippi. Wicker frequently advocates for increased military spending and writes op-eds in The New York Times calling for more shipbuilding. The connection between his political positions and his state's economic interests couldn't be clearer.

Defense contractors understand this leverage and use it effectively. They can threaten lawmakers with the prospect of lost jobs unless they support increased military funding. Lockheed Martin and other contractors can simply state, "We have to have increased funding of this contract or you will lose jobs." This creates a powerful incentive for politicians to maintain or increase military spending, regardless of actual defense needs.

The contractors reinforce this influence through campaign contributions. They donate significant sums to lawmakers who control military spending, ensuring their political support continues. These contributions typically split evenly between Democrats and Republicans, demonstrating that military spending transcends partisan politics when jobs are at stake.

The impact extends beyond individual districts. Major defense projects often involve suppliers and subcontractors spread across multiple states and districts, creating a web of economic dependencies. Cutting funding for a single weapons system could affect jobs in dozens of congressional districts, making such cuts politically toxic.

This strategic distribution of jobs creates what analysts call a "political engineering" system. Contractors don't just build weapons - they build political support by making communities dependent on military spending. The result is a self-perpetuating cycle where military spending becomes essential for local economic survival.

Congressman Mike Rogers provides another clear example of this system. He sits on critical military oversight committees while representing a district receiving billions in defense contracts. He accepts substantial campaign contributions from defense contractors, gets reelected, and continues approving increased military spending. The cycle continues, driven by the connection between jobs, votes, and military budgets.

This reality transforms military spending debates. Rather than focusing on national security needs or cost efficiency, discussions center on protecting local jobs and economies. The system ensures that reducing military spending faces intense political resistance, even when cuts might serve national interests.

Campaign Finance Connections

The flow of money from defense contractors to political campaigns reveals how military spending decisions are shaped by private interests. Lockheed Martin, leading the defense industry, spent $2.7 million on political contributions in a single election cycle, carefully dividing this money between Democrats and Republicans. This figure, significant on its own, represents just the beginning of contractor influence in American politics.

These campaign contributions increase strategically as elections approach. Defense contractors understand that supporting political campaigns provides access and influence over military spending decisions. The money flows to key committee members who oversee defense budgets and military procurement. By contributing to campaigns on both sides of the aisle, contractors ensure their interests remain protected regardless of which party holds power.

The political influence extends beyond direct campaign contributions. Defense contractors invest heavily in showing lawmakers their products and capabilities. They organize demonstrations, facility tours, and briefings, all designed to convince politicians of the need for continued or increased military spending. These activities, combined with campaign contributions, create a powerful system of influence over defense policy.

The numbers tell a compelling story of political investment. Looking at the last 19 years of data on private contractors reveals a consistent pattern of campaign contributions targeting members of key military oversight committees. These lawmakers, responsible for approving military budgets and overseeing procurement programs, receive substantial financial support from the very companies they regulate.

The system becomes even more concerning when examining stock ownership. Some lawmakers who approve military budgets own shares in defense contracting companies. This creates a direct financial incentive to support increased military spending - as the contractors profit, so do the politicians who own their stock. The conflict of interest could hardly be more obvious.

Defense contractors maximize their influence by timing contributions around crucial votes and budget decisions. When major procurement programs come up for review or funding, campaign contributions often spike. This strategic timing helps ensure favorable treatment of contractor interests during critical decision points.

The influence of campaign finance extends to both authorization and oversight functions. Lawmakers who receive contractor contributions may be less inclined to investigate cost overruns or question expensive procurement programs. This creates a system where effective oversight takes a back seat to contractor interests.

Congressional Stock Holdings

One of the most troubling aspects of military spending oversight emerges in the stock portfolios of lawmakers who control the defense budget. Members of Congress who approve military spending and oversee defense contracts often own shares in the very companies they regulate. This means when they vote to increase military budgets or approve expensive weapons programs, they personally profit from these decisions.

This direct financial interest in defense contractors creates an obvious conflict of interest. When lawmakers consider military spending bills, they're not just deciding how to allocate taxpayer money - they're potentially voting to increase the value of their own investment portfolios. The system essentially allows members of Congress to bet on decisions they themselves control.

The impact becomes clear when examining specific procurement programs. When Congress approves billions for new fighter jets, ships, or missile systems, the stock prices of major defense contractors typically rise. Lawmakers holding shares in these companies see their investments grow in value - a direct personal benefit from their official actions.

The scale of these holdings raises serious concerns about objectivity in military oversight. Lawmakers with significant investments in defense companies face an inherent conflict between their duty to protect taxpayer interests and their personal financial stake in contractor profits. This conflict becomes particularly acute during budget negotiations and procurement decisions.

The situation worsens when considering the broader context of military spending oversight. Beyond stock ownership, many of these same lawmakers receive campaign contributions from defense contractors and represent districts with major military facilities. This creates multiple layers of influence all pushing toward increased military spending, regardless of actual defense needs.

Even more concerning, no effective mechanism exists to prevent this conflict of interest. While lawmakers must disclose their stock holdings, they can still vote on matters directly affecting companies they own. This creates a system where personal profit can influence national security decisions.

The relationship between congressional stock holdings and defense contractor influence extends beyond individual lawmakers. Family members of Congress members often hold defense industry stocks as well, creating additional financial ties between those who approve military spending and those who profit from it.

How Contractors Shape Policy

The influence of defense contractors on American military policy represents one of the most sophisticated and effective lobbying operations in history. Through a complex web of political contributions, strategic job creation, revolving door hiring practices, and direct policy influence, these contractors have created a system that virtually guarantees continued growth in military spending, regardless of actual defense needs.

The numbers reveal the scale of this influence. Defense contractors receive 466 billion dollars annually - 54% of the entire defense budget. Lockheed Martin alone gets $47.5 billion per year from the government, exceeding NASA's entire budget. This massive flow of public money creates enormous incentive and resources for contractors to shape the policies that determine military spending.

The contractors' approach to policy influence operates on multiple levels. At the most basic level, they employ traditional lobbying tactics, spending millions on political contributions carefully divided between both major parties. Lockheed Martin, for example, spent $2.7 million on political contributions in a single election cycle, splitting the money evenly between Democrats and Republicans to ensure influence regardless of which party holds power.

However, the contractors' most effective policy-shaping tool lies in their strategic placement of facilities and jobs across congressional districts. They deliberately distribute their operations across dozens of states and political districts, creating what amounts to an economic hostage situation. When military spending cuts are proposed, contractors can threaten job losses in multiple congressional districts simultaneously. No politician wants to be known as the one who caused local unemployment, making it politically impossible to reduce military spending significantly.

The revolving door between the Pentagon and defense contractors creates another powerful channel for policy influence. In 2022 alone, top defense companies hired 672 former Pentagon employees as lobbyists, board members, and executives. These individuals bring intimate knowledge of military planning, budgeting processes, and procurement procedures to their corporate roles. More importantly, they maintain relationships with former colleagues still working in government, creating informal channels of influence over policy decisions.

The case of Jim Mattis illustrates how this revolving door shapes policy. After serving as a military general, Mattis joined General Dynamics' board, then became Secretary of Defense under President Trump, only to return to General Dynamics afterward. This pattern repeats throughout the defense industry, with officials moving between government and contractor roles, each transition building stronger connections between policy makers and defense companies.

Contractors further shape policy through their role as exclusive providers of critical military capabilities. The consolidation from 51 contractors to just five major players has made the Pentagon increasingly dependent on these companies. When only one contractor can produce essential equipment like the F-35 fighter jet, that contractor gains significant influence over military planning and procurement policies. The Pentagon cannot risk alienating these contractors because they've become "too important to fail."

The influence extends to research and development priorities. Contractors help shape which technologies the military pursues, often steering development toward expensive, contractor-friendly solutions rather than more cost-effective alternatives. The $140 billion spent annually on military R&D flows largely through these contractors, giving them substantial influence over the future direction of military technology.

The contractors' policy influence becomes particularly evident in procurement decisions. They've successfully pushed for "cost-plus" contracts that guarantee profits regardless of performance or efficiency. When the Pentagon attempted to implement stricter cost controls, contractors leveraged their political connections and economic influence to resist these reforms.

Geographic strategy plays a crucial role in policy influence. Contractors cluster their offices near the Pentagon in an area literally called "Pentagon City," facilitating constant interaction between corporate and military officials. This physical proximity enables informal influence over policy through daily personal contacts and relationships.

The effectiveness of contractor influence appears in the steady growth of military spending even after major conflicts end. Despite withdrawing from Afghanistan and Iraq, the defense budget continues growing. Contractors have successfully shaped a policy environment where reducing military spending becomes politically impossible, regardless of strategic needs or fiscal constraints.

The impact of this influence extends beyond specific weapons programs or budget items. Contractors shape fundamental assumptions about American military policy, promoting a vision of national security that requires constant increases in military spending. They've created a system where policy decisions often reflect contractor interests rather than strategic requirements or taxpayer concerns.

This sophisticated influence operation has effectively privatized significant aspects of military policy-making. While elected officials and military leaders make formal decisions, contractors shape the context and constraints within which these decisions occur. The result is a policy-making process that consistently favors expensive, contractor-friendly solutions over potentially more effective alternatives.

Chapter Seven

Balancing The Books

Military vs. Domestic Spending

The stark reality of American federal spending becomes clear in a single statistic: almost half of all discretionary federal spending goes to the military. While the defense budget grows to $916 billion, critical domestic programs compete for remaining funds. Education, healthcare, infrastructure, and environmental protection all must share what's left after military spending takes its enormous share.

This spending imbalance reflects clear priorities. The Department of Defense receives about 50% of discretionary funding, while the Department of State - responsible for diplomacy and international relations - receives only 1-2%. This disparity reveals how America prioritizes military solutions over diplomatic ones, despite evidence that diplomacy often proves more effective and far less expensive than military intervention.

The trade-offs become clearer when examining specific numbers. While the military spends $352 billion on operations and maintenance alone, domestic programs struggle for funding. Environmental cleanup of military sites consumes significant resources, yet environmental protection agencies face budget constraints. The Pentagon spends $2.5 billion just to offset increased fuel costs - money that could fund numerous domestic initiatives.

Infrastructure presents a telling comparison. The military maintains 1,250 bases worldwide, including 800 foreign installations, while American bridges, roads, and public facilities deteriorate. The $13.3 billion cost of a single aircraft carrier could rehabilitate numerous domestic infrastructure projects. Even basic maintenance becomes a stark choice - while the military can spend $400,000 to unclog a carrier's toilet, many American communities struggle with aging water systems.

Healthcare spending reveals similar disparities. The military provides comprehensive healthcare coverage for active-duty personnel, costing $39 billion annually.

Meanwhile, many Americans lack basic healthcare access. The military's medical research budget of $1.5 billion produces advances that often benefit civilian medicine, yet many Americans cannot afford basic medical care.

Education funding shows another dimension of this imbalance. While the military offers significant education benefits to service members and their families, public education systems often face resource shortages. The Pentagon can spend $10.7 million to train a single F-35 pilot, while many public schools struggle to maintain basic programs.

The ripple effects of this spending priority extend throughout society. When the military consumes such a large portion of federal resources, it limits investment in scientific research, renewable energy development, poverty reduction, and countless other domestic needs. Even successful military research that produces civilian benefits - like GPS or internet technology - raises questions about whether direct investment in civilian research might prove more efficient.

Recent global events have intensified this domestic-military spending tension. As new security challenges emerge and military spending increases, domestic programs face growing pressure. The military budget's continued growth, approaching one trillion dollars, raises fundamental questions about national priorities and the balance between security and domestic well-being.

The Healthcare Trade-off

The numbers tell a startling story of national priorities. While the Pentagon spends $39 billion annually just for healthcare services for active-duty personnel, millions of Americans lack basic medical coverage. The military healthcare system, one of the world's largest, provides comprehensive coverage for service members and their families, yet over 90 million Americans remain either uninsured or underinsured. This stark contrast raises fundamental questions about how America allocates its resources.

Consider the scale of military healthcare spending. Beyond the $39 billion for active-duty care, the military invests an additional $50 billion in various healthcare costs. This total of nearly $90 billion for military healthcare exceeds the entire military budgets of most nations. Yet despite this massive investment in military medical services, the broader American healthcare system leaves millions struggling to afford basic care.

The irony deepens when examining specific military medical programs. The Pentagon maintains a sophisticated global healthcare network, with medical facilities at bases worldwide. Military personnel receive comprehensive coverage including preventive care, dental services, mental health support, and family care. The system must function everywhere U.S. troops deploy, from major bases to remote outposts, ensuring service members receive high-quality care regardless of location.

Military medical research receives substantial funding - $1.5 billion annually - often producing advances that benefit civilian medicine. These innovations, while valuable, highlight a peculiar dynamic: Americans must wait for military research to trickle down to civilian applications rather than receiving direct investment in public health research. The system prioritizes military medical capabilities over broader public health needs.

The cost comparisons become even more striking at the individual level. While military personnel receive full medical coverage as part of their compensation, many civilian Americans face crushing medical debt. The military can spend $400,000 to repair a toilet system on an aircraft carrier, yet countless Americans must choose between medical care and other basic needs.

This healthcare trade-off extends beyond immediate medical services. The military's $352 billion operations and maintenance budget includes substantial healthcare infrastructure - hospitals, clinics, medical supply chains, and support services. Meanwhile, many American communities lack adequate medical facilities or struggle with aging healthcare infrastructure.

The situation becomes more complex when considering veteran healthcare. The United States spends more on veteran benefits than China, Russia, and India combined.

While this commitment to veteran care is admirable, it raises questions about why similar resources aren't available for the general population. The country demonstrates it can provide comprehensive healthcare when it chooses to do so.

Recent global events have intensified this healthcare divide. As military spending continues growing toward one trillion dollars annually, the pandemic exposed severe weaknesses in America's public health system. The military can maintain medical facilities worldwide for a relatively small portion of its population, while the broader American healthcare system struggles to meet basic needs during crises.

The trade-off appears most starkly in research and development. While the Pentagon pours $140 billion into various R&D programs, including medical research, civilian medical research often faces funding constraints. The military's development of advanced medical technologies and treatments demonstrates America's capability to innovate in healthcare - when it chooses to make the investment.

This disparity in healthcare priorities reflects broader questions about national security. While maintaining military medical capabilities certainly serves strategic interests, the lack of universal healthcare access arguably represents its own security threat. A population's health directly affects national strength and resilience, yet current spending priorities favor military medical capabilities over broader public health.

Education and Infrastructure Needs

While the Pentagon's budget approaches $916 billion, America's educational system and infrastructure face chronic underfunding. The contrast becomes particularly striking when examining specific military expenditures: the $2 trillion F-35 program alone could revolutionize American education, while the $13.3 billion cost of a single aircraft carrier could rebuild countless schools and bridges.

The military's approach to education within its own system demonstrates what's possible with adequate funding. The Department of Defense operates its own school system for service members' children, providing comprehensive education at bases worldwide. These schools receive full funding for facilities, teachers, and resources. Meanwhile, many American public schools struggle with overcrowded classrooms, aging buildings, and limited resources.

Infrastructure spending shows similar disparities. The military maintains 1,250 bases worldwide, including 800 foreign installations, each with sophisticated infrastructure. When the military needs new facilities, funding appears - $85 million for jet fuel tanks in Japan, $75 million for an operations support facility in California. Yet domestic infrastructure continues deteriorating, with bridges, roads, and public facilities desperately needing repair.

The military's construction budget, though the smallest major category at $19 billion, still exceeds many states' entire infrastructure budgets. This money builds and maintains facilities across 80 countries, creating modern infrastructure for military purposes while domestic infrastructure ages. The Pentagon can spend $400,000 to unclog a toilet on an aircraft carrier, yet many

American communities struggle with aging water systems and sewage facilities.

Educational technology presents another stark comparison. While military training programs employ cutting-edge technology - spending $10.7 million to train a single F-35 pilot or $11 million for an F-22 pilot - many American schools lack basic computer resources. The military's $140 billion research and development budget produces technological advances that could benefit education, yet these innovations often remain confined to military applications.

The infrastructure gap becomes particularly evident in transportation systems. The military operates 800 transport aircraft and 450 aerial refueling tankers, maintaining a sophisticated global logistics network. Moving an Armored Brigade Combat Team one mile costs $66,000 in fuel and maintenance, yet domestic transportation infrastructure receives fraction of such investment. The country can transport military equipment worldwide but struggles to maintain basic transportation systems at home.

Training and development reveal additional contrasts. The military spends approximately $50,000 to transform a civilian into a trained infantry soldier, investing another $17,000 in their individual equipment. Meanwhile, many American teachers must purchase basic classroom supplies with their own money, and students often lack essential learning materials.

Recent global events have heightened these disparities. As military spending continues growing toward one trillion dollars, domestic education and infrastructure needs become more acute. The pandemic exposed weaknesses in educational infrastructure, particularly in digital learning capabilities, while climate change stresses aging physical infrastructure. Yet military spending continues increasing while domestic investment lags.

The military's own infrastructure challenges ironically highlight domestic needs. The Pentagon must invest in protecting bases from climate change impacts, particularly coastal installations threatened by rising seas. These same environmental threats endanger civilian infrastructure, yet resources for civilian climate adaptation remain limited.

These spending priorities raise fundamental questions about national security and strength. While military capability certainly contributes to national security, deteriorating domestic infrastructure and educational systems arguably pose their own security threats. A country's strength depends not just on military power but on educated citizens and functional infrastructure.

Environmental Impact and Cleanup Costs

The environmental footprint of America's military machine extends far beyond combat operations. Hidden within the Pentagon's $352 billion operations and maintenance budget lies a costly reality: massive environmental cleanup operations for areas where the military has left unexploded ordnance or spilled hazardous chemicals into local environments. This environmental burden represents a largely unseen cost of military operations.

The scale of military fuel consumption alone creates significant environmental challenges. The Pentagon spends $2.5 billion just to offset increased fuel costs, highlighting the military's massive carbon footprint. Each hour of F-35 flight costs $35,000, much of that tied to fuel consumption. Moving an Armored Brigade Combat Team one mile requires $66,000 in fuel and maintenance, demonstrating how routine military operations contribute to environmental impacts.

Climate change has forced the military to confront environmental realities directly. Military bases, particularly in coastal areas like Guam, require extensive infrastructure improvements to combat rising sea levels. The Defense Department now identifies climate change as a major threat to military readiness, requiring substantial investment in facility protection and adaptation.

The 1,250 military bases worldwide, including 800 foreign installations, all require environmental management. Each base must handle waste disposal, manage hazardous materials, and maintain environmental compliance. When bases close or operations relocate, the military often faces extensive cleanup requirements for contaminated soil and water.

The military's attempts to address these environmental challenges reflect in its research and development priorities. Part of the $140 billion R&D budget now goes toward developing renewable energy systems and more efficient technologies. This investment acknowledges that environmental sustainability affects military capability and long-term costs.

Infrastructure adaptations for climate change consume increasing resources. The military must modify or relocate facilities threatened by rising seas, extreme weather, and other environmental impacts. These adaptations compete for funding with other military priorities, demonstrating how environmental costs affect overall military capabilities.

The environmental impact extends to local communities near military installations. Cleanup operations often take decades and cost billions, affecting water supplies, soil quality, and public health. While the military budget includes funds for environmental remediation, the full cost of environmental damage often exceeds allocated resources.

Recent military planning increasingly incorporates environmental considerations. The Pentagon now views climate change as a threat multiplier that could intensify conflicts and create new security challenges. This recognition drives investment in both environmental protection and adaptation strategies, though critics argue these efforts remain insufficient given the scale of military environmental impacts.

The Cost of Global Security

The United States pays an extraordinary price for its role as global security provider. At $916 billion and climbing toward one trillion dollars, the military budget reflects America's unique position as the world's policeman - a role that involves maintaining order across every corner of the globe. This isn't just about defending American territory; it's about enforcing rules and maintaining a global system that America created and from which it benefits immensely.

The numbers behind this global security role are staggering. The U.S. maintains approximately 750 military bases across 80 countries, creating what amounts to a worldwide empire built on cooperation rather than conquest. The Navy patrols global shipping lanes through which 80% of world trade by volume and 70% by value travels. This naval presence alone costs billions annually but ensures the free flow of international commerce.

Consider the specific costs of maintaining this global presence. Four aircraft carriers remain continuously deployed worldwide, each deployment costing upwards of $46 million annually. The military spent $85 million for jet fuel tanks in Japan and maintains forces near China, Russia, and other potential adversaries. In the Pacific region alone, the U.S. allocated $6.1 billion for operations, including $1.8 billion for modernizing facilities and $2.3 billion for training exercises.

The human cost of global security appears in personnel expenses. The military employs 3.4 million people, including 1.3 million active-duty service members and 800,000 reservists. Supporting these personnel worldwide requires extensive infrastructure - from housing and healthcare to schools and recreation facilities. Even maintaining American-style grocery stores and restaurants at overseas bases adds significant costs to the global security mission.

This global presence serves multiple functions beyond combat capability. The military provides disaster relief, humanitarian assistance, and emergency response worldwide. It maintains sophisticated early warning systems, missile defense networks, and communication infrastructure that benefit allies and partners. These non-combat roles add substantially to the cost of global security but are considered essential for maintaining international stability.

However, this approach to global security creates its own paradox. As the U.S. expands its military capabilities, other nations feel compelled to increase their own military spending. China and Russia respond to American military presence by developing new weapons systems, creating an arms race that drives costs ever higher. The U.S. then must spend more to maintain its technological edge, perpetuating a cycle of increasing military expenditure.

The financial burden of global security extends beyond direct military spending. The U.S. provides substantial security assistance to allies and partners, funds infrastructure improvements in strategic locations, and maintains diplomatic support structures worldwide. These auxiliary costs, often overlooked in military budget discussions, form an integral part of America's global security strategy.

Critics argue this level of spending on global security comes at the expense of domestic needs. While the military budget approaches one trillion dollars, American communities struggle with inadequate healthcare, education, and infrastructure. The question becomes whether maintaining such extensive global security capabilities truly serves national interests when domestic challenges remain unaddressed.

Chapter Eight

Future Perspectives

The Rising Budget Trend

The trajectory of American military spending tells a story of relentless growth. From $850 billion in 2022 to $916 billion in 2023, the defense budget continues its steady march toward the trillion-dollar threshold. Despite the end of major conflicts in Afghanistan and Iraq, despite withdrawal from active combat zones, and despite periods of relative peace, military spending continues its upward climb, defying normal expectations of post-war reduction.

This persistent growth reflects multiple driving forces. At the most basic level, the military must maintain its vast global infrastructure - 1,250 bases worldwide, including 800 foreign installations across 80 countries. Just maintaining this existing network requires ever-increasing funding. Inflation alone demanded $12.6 billion in additional funding for 2023, with $3.8 billion dedicated solely to covering increased construction labor costs and $2.5 billion allocated just to offset rising fuel prices.

The procurement cycle drives substantial budget growth. The military continues purchasing expensive new weapons systems while maintaining existing equipment. In 2023, this meant buying 77 new jets at $142 million each, then requesting another $14 billion for 83 more. The Navy spent $7.3 billion on two Virginia-class submarines and $5.6 billion on two Arleigh Burke destroyers. Each new system adds to future maintenance and operating costs, creating a perpetual cycle of increasing expenses.

Personnel costs contribute significantly to budget growth. The military must offer competitive salaries and benefits to maintain its all-volunteer force, leading to steady increases in personnel spending. The $172 billion personnel budget covers pay, benefits, retirement, and healthcare for 3.4 million people, including 1.3 million active-duty service members and 800,000 reservists. These costs consistently rise faster than inflation.

Research and development demands ever-larger investments to maintain technological superiority. The current $140 billion R&D budget funds everything from artificial intelligence to autonomous systems, from laser weapons to exoskeletons. As potential adversaries like China advance their own military technology, maintaining America's technological edge requires increasing investment in new capabilities.

The defense industry's structure virtually guarantees rising costs. With only five major contractors controlling most military production, limited competition allows companies to charge premium prices. A missile that once cost $25,000 now approaches half a million dollars. The Pentagon pays $3,357 for parts available elsewhere for $15. These inflated costs, combined with continuous procurement, create persistent upward pressure on the overall budget.

International commitments drive further spending increases. The Pacific region alone received $6.1 billion for operations in 2023, including $1.8 billion for modernizing facilities and $2.3 billion for training exercises. European operations required $4.2 billion, while Middle East operations, though reduced, still consumed $27.3 billion. Each global commitment demands ongoing investment in facilities, personnel, and equipment.

Climate change creates new spending requirements. Military bases, particularly coastal installations, need extensive modifications to combat rising sea levels and extreme weather. These environmental adaptations represent new costs above traditional military spending, forcing budget increases just to maintain existing capabilities.

The political dynamics surrounding military spending ensure continued growth. Defense contractors strategically locate facilities across congressional districts, making spending cuts politically difficult. Campaign contributions from defense companies influence lawmakers' decisions. The revolving door between the Pentagon and defense contractors creates a system that consistently pushes for higher spending.

Even accounting failures contribute to budget growth. The Pentagon has never successfully passed an audit, with 61% of its physical assets effectively missing from tracking systems. This lack of accountability leads to redundant purchases and inefficient spending, creating pressure for larger budgets to compensate for poor asset management.

Looking ahead, multiple factors suggest continued budget growth. New security challenges, technological competition with China, modernization requirements, and ongoing global commitments all point toward increased spending. The trillion-dollar threshold appears not as a ceiling but as another milestone in the continuing expansion of American military spending.

China's Military Growth

The rise of Chinese military power represents one of the primary drivers of American defense spending. While the U.S. military budget reaches $916 billion, China spends approximately $230 billion annually on its armed forces - making it the world's second-largest military spender, yet still spending only about a quarter of what America does. However, these raw numbers mask a more complex and concerning reality about China's military expansion.

Major General Cameron Holt from the U.S. Air Force's Acquisition, Technology, and Logistics Office revealed a startling truth: China gets far more military capability per dollar than the United States. For every dollar China spends, the U.S. must spend $20 to achieve the same capability. This purchasing power disparity means China's $230 billion effectively buys as much military capability as several trillion dollars of American spending, creating a serious challenge to U.S. military superiority.

China's nuclear arsenal demonstrates this growing challenge. Current estimates place China's nuclear stockpile between 400 and 500 warheads, but the Pentagon projects this number will reach 1,500 by 2035. This dramatic expansion would bring China's nuclear capabilities in line with those of Russia and the United States, fundamentally altering the global strategic balance and potentially triggering a new nuclear arms race.

The Chinese military's approach to personnel costs provides another advantage. While America maintains an all-volunteer force with competitive salaries and benefits, Chinese military personnel receive significantly lower compensation. China spends just $1,500 to equip each infantry soldier, compared to America's $17,000 per soldier. This cost difference allows China to maintain a larger force structure while investing more in modernization and expansion.

China's shipbuilding capacity has become particularly concerning for U.S. military planners. While American shipyards struggle to meet construction schedules for Virginia-class submarines and other vessels, China's shipbuilding industry produces naval vessels at what the Pentagon describes as a "breakneck speed." This production capability allows China to expand its navy rapidly while America struggles to maintain its fleet size.

Training represents another area where China is closing the gap. While American pilots typically log 200 flight hours annually, Chinese pilots now achieve 100-110 hours per year. Though still less than U.S. training levels, this represents a significant improvement in Chinese capabilities. Similar advances appear across all branches of China's military, indicating a comprehensive effort to improve force quality while expanding quantity.

China's military modernization extends beyond conventional forces. The country invests heavily in advanced technologies, including artificial intelligence, hypersonic weapons, and space-based systems. While America pioneered many of these technologies, China's approach of waiting until others perfect new capabilities before reverse-engineering them saves substantial development costs while still achieving advanced capabilities.

The Belt and Road Initiative represents China's alternative approach to global influence. Rather than maintaining hundreds of overseas military bases like the United States, China uses infrastructure projects and economic partnerships to expand its influence. This strategy often achieves similar strategic objectives at lower cost than America's military-centered approach.

Looking ahead, China's military trajectory suggests continued rapid growth in capabilities. The country's defense industry, though less technologically advanced than America's, demonstrates increasing sophistication. Chinese weapons systems, once considered inferior copies of Western equipment, now incorporate innovative features and capabilities that concern U.S. military planners.

This growth in Chinese military power drives significant American spending decisions. The U.S. Navy's focus on new ship construction, the Air Force's investment in advanced aircraft, and the Pentagon's emphasis on maintaining technological superiority all reflect responses to China's military expansion. As China continues growing its military capabilities, pressure increases for America to spend more to maintain its advantages.

The competition extends into new domains like cyber warfare and space operations. China's investments in these areas force corresponding American expenditures to maintain capabilities in these crucial future battlespaces. The result is a technology race that drives both nations to increase military spending continuously.

Understanding China's military growth becomes crucial for evaluating American defense spending. As China achieves greater military capabilities while spending less, questions arise about the efficiency and sustainability of America's approach to military expenditure. The challenge lies not just in spending more, but in spending more effectively to maintain military advantages in an increasingly competitive environment.

Modern Security Challenges

Today's security landscape presents complexities far beyond traditional military threats. As America's military budget approaches one trillion dollars, the nature of security challenges has evolved dramatically, creating new demands that test both military capabilities and spending priorities. These modern challenges range from conventional military competition to emerging technological threats, from climate change to cyber warfare.

The rise of multi-domain threats represents perhaps the most significant shift in security challenges. China, identified as America's foremost strategic competitor, presents what the National Defense Strategy calls a "growing multi-domain threat." This means potential confrontation across land, sea, air, space, and cyberspace simultaneously - a challenge America hasn't faced since the Cold War. Meeting this comprehensive threat requires massive investment across all military domains.

Nuclear proliferation creates another layer of modern security concerns. As countries like North Korea maintain nuclear capabilities and Iran potentially develops them, the U.S. spends approximately $16 billion annually just maintaining its nuclear arsenal. The modernization of nuclear forces, including programs like the Sentinel ICBM system at $96 billion, reflects the continuing importance of nuclear deterrence in modern security.

Technological warfare has emerged as a crucial battleground. The Pentagon invests heavily in artificial intelligence, autonomous systems, and advanced computing capabilities. The military spends $140 billion on research and development, including AI systems for analyzing drone footage, autonomous submarines, and laser weapons. Yet potential adversaries often wait for America to perfect these technologies before reverse-engineering them at lower cost.

Cyber security presents an entirely new dimension of military challenges. Modern weapons systems contain millions of lines of code - the F-35 alone has 8 million lines for basic operations and another 16 million for diagnostic systems. Protecting these complex systems from cyber attacks while maintaining offensive cyber capabilities requires substantial ongoing investment.

Climate change has become a recognized security threat, forcing military adaptation. Bases face rising sea levels and extreme weather events, requiring expensive infrastructure modifications. The Pentagon must also prepare for potential conflicts driven by climate-related resource scarcity and population displacement. Even basic operations feel the impact - the military spent $2.5 billion just offsetting increased fuel costs in one year.

Asymmetric warfare continues evolving, as demonstrated in Ukraine. The conflict shows how relatively inexpensive drones and precision weapons can challenge sophisticated military forces. America must maintain expensive conventional capabilities while also developing countermeasures against low-cost threats. The military spent $812 million just replacing GMLRS rockets provided to Ukraine.

Global power competition has returned as a primary security challenge. Russia's actions in Ukraine and China's military expansion create a complex strategic environment requiring constant military presence worldwide. Maintaining this presence through 800 overseas bases across 80 countries consumes enormous resources but remains crucial for deterring potential adversaries.

The proliferation of advanced weapons technology poses another modern challenge. Countries previously limited to basic military capabilities now access sophisticated weapons systems. The U.S. must maintain technological superiority across a broader spectrum of potential adversaries, driving increased investment in research and development.

Maritime security challenges grow more complex as international commerce expands. The U.S. Navy patrols shipping lanes carrying 80% of global trade volume and 70% of value. Protecting these vital economic arteries requires maintaining expensive naval capabilities, including 11 aircraft carriers costing $13.3 billion each.

Traditional threats haven't disappeared but have evolved. While preparing for high-technology warfare, the military must maintain capabilities against conventional forces and irregular opponents. This requirement for full-spectrum dominance drives much of the current military budget growth.

These diverse security challenges create competing demands for limited resources. The military must balance investment in emerging capabilities against maintaining traditional forces, modernizing nuclear deterrence while developing cyber defenses, all while managing the impact of climate change on military infrastructure.

Reforming Military Spending

The challenge of reforming military spending collides with a deeply entrenched system that actively resists change. With the Pentagon failing six consecutive years of independent audits and 61% of military assets effectively missing from tracking systems, the need for reform is clear. Yet the complex web of political interests, contractor influence, and institutional momentum makes meaningful change extraordinarily difficult.

The most glaring issue demanding reform is the Pentagon's inability to track its own spending and assets. When professional accountants attempt to audit military expenditures, they encounter a system so complex and disorganized that they cannot complete their task. This lack of basic financial accountability means the military likely purchases equipment it already owns simply because it can't locate existing inventory. Any serious reform must start with establishing fundamental financial controls and asset tracking.

The relationship between defense contractors and the military requires dramatic restructuring. The consolidation from 51 contractors to just five major players has created effective monopolies in military procurement. When the Pentagon needs new equipment, it often faces a single bidder, eliminating competitive pressure to control costs. The result appears in price inflation that defies logic - a $15 ball bearing costing $3,357, or a $25,000 missile now priced at half a million dollars.

The revolving door between the Pentagon and defense contractors demands immediate attention. In 2022 alone, defense companies hired 672 former Pentagon employees as lobbyists, board members, and executives. This constant flow of personnel between government and contractors creates conflicts of interest and undermines efforts to control costs. Reform must include stricter controls on post-government employment in the defense industry.

Congressional oversight needs fundamental reform. Currently, lawmakers who approve military budgets often own stock in defense contractors, creating direct financial incentives to increase military spending. Defense contractors contribute heavily to political campaigns and strategically locate facilities across congressional districts to make spending cuts politically impossible. Any meaningful reform must address these political influences on military spending decisions.

The procurement system itself requires complete overhaul. The current "cost-plus" contracting system, where contractors receive guaranteed profits regardless of performance, encourages inefficiency and waste. Reform should introduce stronger incentives for cost control and performance, possibly including fixed-price contracts and penalties for cost overruns.

Research and development spending needs better focus and oversight. While the military's $140 billion R&D budget produces valuable innovations, many projects fail to deliver practical results. Reform should emphasize practical capabilities over theoretical advantages and require more rigorous evaluation of research programs' potential benefits.

The global base network, consisting of 1,250 installations including 800 overseas bases, demands careful review. While global presence serves strategic purposes, maintaining such extensive infrastructure consumes enormous resources. Reform should evaluate which bases truly serve current strategic needs versus historical momentum.

Personnel costs require careful reconsideration. Despite spending $172 billion annually on military personnel, many service members qualify for food stamps. Reform must address this disparity, ensuring resources actually reach service members while controlling overall personnel costs.

Environmental costs need greater attention in reform efforts. The military's environmental impact includes unexploded ordnance, chemical contamination, and massive carbon emissions. Reform should incorporate environmental costs into procurement decisions and operational planning, potentially driving more sustainable practices.

The challenge of reform extends beyond simple cost-cutting. America's global security responsibilities require substantial military capability. However, the current system's inefficiencies and misaligned incentives waste resources while potentially undermining military effectiveness. True reform must balance maintaining necessary capabilities with eliminating waste and inefficiency.

The Road to One Trillion

America's military budget stands at a historic crossroads. From $850 billion in 2022 to $916 billion in 2023, defense spending marches inexorably toward the trillion-dollar threshold. This trajectory isn't just about numbers - it represents a fundamental transformation in how America funds its military power and defines its global role.

The path to one trillion dollars follows clear patterns. Annual increases consistently outpace inflation, with the 2023 budget requiring $12.6 billion just to offset inflation's impact. Basic operational costs continue rising - $2.5 billion solely for increased fuel costs, $3.8 billion for construction labor inflation. These underlying cost pressures create momentum toward higher spending regardless of strategic needs.

Major weapons programs drive substantial spending increases. The F-35 program alone will cost $2 trillion over its lifetime. Each new aircraft carrier demands $13.3 billion. The military plans to buy 83 new jets at $142 million each, 600 cruise missiles at $1.6 million apiece, and thousands of combat vehicles at $372,000 each. Every procurement decision adds to long-term maintenance and operating costs.

The consolidation of the defense industry ensures continuing cost inflation. With only five major contractors controlling most military production, competitive pressure to control costs has virtually disappeared. A missile that once cost $25,000 now approaches half a million dollars. Parts available for $15 cost $3,357 when purchased through defense contractors. These inflated prices multiply across thousands of components and systems.

Global commitments require ever-increasing investment. Maintaining 800 overseas bases across 80 countries demands constant funding increases. The Pacific region alone receives $6.1 billion for operations, while European operations require $4.2 billion. Middle

East operations, though reduced, still consume $27.3 billion. Each global commitment generates its own spending momentum.

Personnel costs continue rising as the military competes for talent. The current $172 billion personnel budget must grow to maintain competitive salaries and benefits for 3.4 million service members and civilian employees. Specialized positions command additional premiums - the military spent $28 million in one year just hiring artificial intelligence experts.

Research and development demands increasingly larger investments. The current $140 billion R&D budget funds everything from artificial intelligence to autonomous weapons, from laser systems to advanced materials. As potential adversaries advance their capabilities, maintaining technological superiority requires ever-greater spending.

Environmental challenges create new spending requirements. Military bases need protection from rising seas and extreme weather. Environmental cleanup of contaminated sites demands ongoing investment. These climate-related costs add another layer of spending pressure previously absent from military budgets.

The political system virtually guarantees continued spending growth. Defense contractors maintain facilities across congressional districts, making spending cuts politically toxic. The revolving door between the Pentagon and contractors ensures strong advocacy for increased budgets. Campaign contributions from defense companies influence legislative decisions about military spending.

As the trillion-dollar threshold approaches, fundamental questions emerge about sustainability and effectiveness. The military's failure to pass basic audits suggests significant waste within current spending. The Pentagon cannot account for 61% of its physical assets, yet continues receiving budget increases. This lack of accountability raises concerns about how effectively additional funding will be used.

Yet global security challenges seem to demand continued investment. China's military modernization, Russia's aggression, emerging technologies, and evolving threats all create pressure for increased capabilities. The question becomes not whether America will spend a trillion dollars on its military, but how soon it will happen and what that massive investment will actually buy.

Conclusion

As we reach the end of this journey through the labyrinth of U.S. military spending, one thing becomes crystal clear: this is not just about numbers. It's about priorities, accountability, and the values we hold as a society.

The trillion-dollar threshold is more than just a financial milestone—it's a reflection of a system unchecked, a machine fueled by secrecy, inefficiency, and the unchecked influence of a powerful few. Year after year, the military-industrial complex grows larger, feeding on tax dollars that could transform lives if redirected toward education, healthcare, infrastructure, or combating climate change.

But the true cost of this spending isn't just financial. It's the erosion of trust in government institutions. It's the opportunity lost for future generations. It's the normalization of a world where a bolt costs $3,357 and $400,000 is spent fixing a clogged toilet, while countless Americans struggle to make ends meet.

This book isn't meant to leave you in despair. It's meant to ignite a spark of awareness. The problems may seem insurmountable, but change begins with knowledge. When citizens understand where their money is going—and why—they gain the power to demand accountability. Transparency is the first step toward reform, and it's something we can achieve if enough voices call for it.

The path to a trillion dollars doesn't have to lead to waste and inefficiency. It can lead to innovation, security, and a better future—but only if we take a hard look at the system, confront the hard truths, and refuse to accept the status quo.

This is your call to action. You've followed the money. Now it's time to follow the questions. Ask your leaders why. Demand answers. Advocate for change. Because at the heart of every dollar spent is a choice—a choice about the kind of nation we want to be.

The trillion-dollar question is this: Will we continue down this path, or will we forge a new one? The answer is up to all of us.

www.ingramcontent.com/pod-product-compliance
Lightning Source LLC
Chambersburg PA
CBHW071026240526
45469CB00006BD/2104